# It's another great book from CGP...

This book is for anyone doing the **AQA Level 1/Level 2 Certificate in Biology**.

It's got clear, concise revision notes covering everything you'll need to do well
in the exams.  What's more, we've included a **free** Online Edition so that
you can revise on a computer or tablet — wherever you are.

## How to get your free Online Edition

Just go to **cgpbooks.co.uk/extras** and enter this code...

3545 2170 5570 3493

By the way, this code only works for one person.  If somebody else has used
this book before you, they might have already claimed the Online Edition.

## CGP — still the best! ☺

Our sole aim here at CGP is to produce the highest
quality books — carefully written, immaculately presented
and dangerously close to being funny.

Then we work our socks off to get them
out to you — at the cheapest possible prices.

# Contents

Published by CGP

From original material by Richard Parsons.

Editors:
Jane Applegarth, Charlotte Burrows, Jane Ellingham, Camilla Simson,
Hayley Thompson, Karen Wells.

Contributors:
Paddy Gannon, Gemma Hallam

ISBN: 978 1 84762 446 8

With thanks to Janet Cruse-Sawyer and Jo Sharrock for the proofreading.
With thanks to Anna Lupton for the copyright research.

Groovy website: www.cgpbooks.co.uk

Printed by Elanders Ltd, Newcastle upon Tyne.
Jolly bits of clipart from CorelDRAW®

# How Science Works

You need to know a few things about the scientific process.  First up is <u>how science works</u> — or how a scientist's <u>mad idea</u> turns into a <u>widely accepted theory</u>.

## Scientists Come Up with Hypotheses — Then Test Them

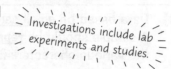

Hundreds of years ago, we thought demons caused illness.

1) Scientists try to <u>explain</u> things.  Everything.

2) They start by <u>observing</u> something they don't understand — it could be anything, e.g. planets in the sky, a person suffering from an illness, what matter is made of... anything.

3) Then, they come up with a <u>hypothesis</u> — a <u>possible explanation</u> for what they've observed.  Scientists can sometimes form a <u>model</u> too — a <u>simplified description</u> or <u>representation</u> of what's physically going on.

4) The next step is to <u>test</u> whether the hypothesis might be <u>right or not</u> — this involves <u>gathering evidence</u> (i.e. <u>data</u> from <u>investigations</u>).

5) The scientist uses the hypothesis to make a <u>prediction</u> — a statement based on the hypothesis that can be <u>tested</u>.  They then <u>carry out an investigation</u>.

*Investigations include lab experiments and studies.*

6) If data from experiments or studies <u>backs up the prediction</u>, you're one step closer to figuring out if the hypothesis is true.

## Other Scientists Will Test the Hypothesis Too

1) <u>Other</u> scientists will use the hypothesis to make their <u>own predictions</u>, and carry out their <u>own experiments</u> or studies.

2) They'll also try to <u>reproduce</u> the original investigations to check the results.

3) And if <u>all the experiments</u> in the world back up the hypothesis, then scientists start to think it's <u>true</u>.

4) However, if a scientist somewhere in the world does an experiment that <u>doesn't</u> fit with the hypothesis (and other scientists can <u>reproduce</u> these results), then the hypothesis is in trouble.

5) When this happens, scientists have to come up with a new hypothesis (maybe a <u>modification</u> of the old hypothesis, or maybe a completely <u>new</u> one).

Then we thought it was caused by 'bad blood' (and treated it with leeches).

## If Evidence Supports a Hypothesis, It's Accepted — for Now

1) If pretty much every scientist in the world believes a hypothesis to be true because experiments back it up, then it usually goes in the <u>textbooks</u> for students to learn.

Now we know many illnesses are due to microorganisms.

2) Accepted hypotheses are often referred to as <u>theories</u>.

3) Our <u>currently accepted</u> theories are the ones that have survived this 'trial by evidence' — they've been tested many, many times over the years and survived (while the less good ones have been ditched).

4) However... they never, <u>never</u> become hard and fast, totally indisputable <u>fact</u>.  You can never know... it'd only take <u>one</u> odd, totally inexplicable result, and the hypothesising and testing would start all over again.

## You expect me to believe that — then show me the evidence...

If scientists think something is true, they need to produce evidence to convince others — it's all part of <u>testing a hypothesis</u>.  One hypothesis might survive these tests, while others won't — it's how things progress.  And along the way some hypotheses will be disproved — i.e. shown not to be true.

# Your Data's Got To Be Good

Evidence is the key to science — but not all evidence is equally good.
The way evidence is gathered can have a big effect on how trustworthy it is...

## Lab Experiments and Studies Are Better Than Rumour

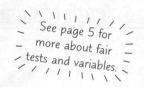
See page 5 for more about fair tests and variables.

1) Results from experiments in laboratories are great. A lab is the easiest place to control variables so that they're all kept constant (except for the one you're investigating). This makes it easier to carry out a FAIR TEST.

2) For things that you can't investigate in the lab (e.g. climate) you conduct scientific studies. As many of the variables as possible are controlled, to make it a fair test.

3) Old wives' tales, rumours, hearsay, "what someone said", and so on, should be taken with a pinch of salt. Without any evidence they're NOT scientific — they're just opinions.

## The Bigger the Sample Size the Better

1) Data based on small samples isn't as good as data based on large samples. A sample should be representative of the whole population (i.e. it should share as many of the various characteristics in the population as possible) — a small sample can't do that as well.

2) The bigger the sample size the better, but scientists have to be realistic when choosing how big. For example, if you were studying how lifestyle affects people's weight it'd be great to study everyone in the UK (a huge sample), but it'd take ages and cost a bomb. Studying a thousand people is more realistic.

## Evidence Needs to be Repeatable and Reproducible

You can have confidence in the results if they can be repeated (during the same experiment) AND other scientists can reproduce them too (in other experiments). If the results aren't repeatable or reproducible, you can't believe them.

The data must be repeatable, and reproducible by others.

If the results are repeatable and reproducible, they're said to be reliable.

EXAMPLE: In 1998, a scientist claimed that he'd found a link between the MMR vaccine (for measles, mumps and rubella) and autism. As a result, many parents stopped their children from having the vaccine — which led to a big rise in the number of children catching measles. However, no other scientist has been able to repeat the results since. Health authorities have now concluded that the vaccine is safe to use.

## Evidence Also Needs to Be Valid

VALID means the data is repeatable, reproducible AND answers the original question.

EXAMPLE: DO POWER LINES CAUSE CANCER?
Some studies have found that children who live near overhead power lines are more likely to develop cancer. What they'd actually found was a correlation (relationship) between the variables "presence of power lines" and "incidence of cancer" — they found that as one changed, so did the other. But this evidence is not enough to say that the power lines cause cancer, as other explanations might be possible. For example, power lines are often near busy roads, so the areas tested could contain different levels of pollution from traffic. So these studies don't show a definite link and so don't answer the original question.

## Repeat after me — repeatable and reproducible = great data...

By now you should have realised how important trustworthy evidence is (even more important than a good supply of spot cream). Unfortunately, you need to know loads more about fair tests and experiments — see p. 5-10.

# Bias and Issues Created by Science

It isn't all hunky-dory in the world of science — there are some problems...

## Scientific Evidence can be Presented in a Biased Way

1) People who want to make a point can sometimes present data in a biased way, e.g. they overemphasise a relationship in the data. (Sometimes without knowing they're doing it.)

2) And there are all sorts of reasons why people might want to do this — for example...

- They want to keep the organisation or company that's funding the research happy. (If the results aren't what they'd like they might not give them any more money to fund further research.)
- Governments might want to persuade voters, other governments, journalists, etc.
- Companies might want to 'big up' their products. Or make impressive safety claims.
- Environmental campaigners might want to persuade people to behave differently.

## Things can Affect How Seriously Evidence is Taken

1) If an investigation is done by a team of highly-regarded scientists it's sometimes taken more seriously than evidence from less well known scientists.

2) But having experience, authority or a fancy qualification doesn't necessarily mean the evidence is good — the only way to tell is to look at the evidence scientifically (i.e. is it valid).

3) Also, some evidence might be ignored if it could create political problems, or emphasised if it helps a particular cause.

EXAMPLE: Some governments were pretty slow to accept the fact that human activities are causing global warming, despite all the evidence. This is because accepting it means they've got to do something about it, which costs money and could hurt their economy. This could lose them a lot of votes.

## Scientific Developments are Great, but they can Raise Issues

Scientific knowledge is increased by doing experiments. And this knowledge leads to scientific developments, e.g. new technologies or new advice. These developments can create issues though. For example:

**Economic issues:** Society can't always afford to do things scientists recommend (e.g. investing heavily in alternative energy sources) without cutting back elsewhere.

**Social issues:** Decisions based on scientific evidence affect people — e.g. should junk food be taxed more highly (to encourage people to eat healthily)? Should alcohol be banned (to prevent health problems)? Would the effect on people's lifestyles be acceptable...

**Environmental issues:** Genetically modified crops may help us produce more food — but some people think they could cause environmental problems (see page 77).

**Ethical issues:** There are a lot of things that scientific developments have made possible, but should we do them? E.g. cloning humans.

## Trust me — I've got a BSc, PhD, PC, TV and a DVD...

We all tend to swoon at people in authority, but you have to ignore that fact and look at the evidence (just because someone has got a whacking great list of letters after their name doesn't mean the evidence is good). Spotting biased evidence isn't the easiest thing in the world — ask yourself 'Does the scientist (or the person writing about it) stand to gain something (or lose something)?' If they do, it's possible that it could be biased.

# Science Has Limits

Science can give us amazing things — cures for diseases, space travel, heated toilet seats...
But science has its limitations — there are questions that it just can't answer.

## Some Questions Are Unanswered by Science — So Far

1) We don't understand everything. And we never will. We'll find out more, for sure — as more hypotheses are suggested, and more experiments are done. But there'll always be stuff we don't know.

> **EXAMPLES:**
> * Today we don't know as much as we'd like about the impacts of global warming.
>   How much will sea level rise? And to what extent will weather patterns change?
> * We also don't know anywhere near as much as we'd like about the Universe.
>   Are there other life forms out there? And what is the Universe made of?

2) These are complicated questions. At the moment scientists don't all agree on the answers because there isn't enough valid evidence.

3) But eventually, we probably will be able to answer these questions once and for all...
All we need is more evidence.

4) But by then there'll be loads of new questions to answer.

## Other Questions Are Unanswerable by Science

1) Then there's the other type... questions that all the experiments in the world won't help us answer — the "Should we be doing this at all?" type questions. There are always two sides...

2) Take embryo screening (which allows you to choose an embryo with particular characteristics).
It's possible to do it — but does that mean we should?

3) Different people have different opinions.

> For example...
> * Some people say it's good... couples whose existing child needs a bone marrow transplant, but who can't find a donor, will be able to have another child selected for its matching bone marrow. This would save the life of their first child — and if they want another child anyway... where's the harm?
> * Other people say it's bad... they say it could have serious effects on the new child. In the above example, the new child might feel unwanted — thinking they were only brought into the world to help someone else. And would they have the right to refuse to donate their bone marrow (as anyone else would)?

4) The question of whether something is morally or ethically right or wrong can't be answered by more experiments — there is no "right" or "wrong" answer.

5) The best we can do is get a consensus from society — a judgement that most people are more or less happy to live by. Science can provide more information to help people make this judgement, and the judgement might change over time. But in the end it's up to people and their conscience.

## Chips or rice? — totally unanswerable by science...

Right — get this straight in your head — science can't tell you whether you should or shouldn't do something. That kind of thing is up to you and society to decide. There are tons of questions that science might be able to answer in the future — like how much sea level might rise due to global warming, what the Universe is made of and whatever happened to those pink stripy socks with Santa on that I used to have.

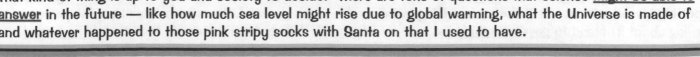

# Designing Investigations

Real <u>scientists</u> need to know <u>how to plan</u> and <u>carry out</u> scientific experiments. Unluckily for you, those pesky examiners think <u>you</u> should be able to do the same — so you'll have <u>questions on experiments</u> in your exams. Don't worry though, these next seven pages have <u>loads of information</u> to help you out.

## Investigations Produce Evidence to Support or Disprove a Hypothesis

1) Scientists <u>observe</u> things and come up with <u>hypotheses</u> to explain them (see page 1).

2) To figure out whether a hypothesis might be correct or not you need to do an <u>investigation</u> to <u>gather some evidence</u>.

3) The first step is to use the hypothesis to come up with a <u>prediction</u> — a statement about what you <u>think will happen</u> that you can <u>test</u>.

4) For example, if the <u>hypothesis</u> is:

> "Spots are caused by picking your nose too much."

Then the <u>prediction</u> might be:

> "People who pick their nose more often will have more spots."

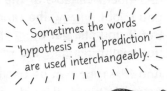

*Sometimes the words 'hypothesis' and 'prediction' are used interchangeably.*

5) Investigations are used to see if there are <u>patterns</u> or <u>relationships between two variables</u>. For example, to see if there's a pattern or relationship between the variables 'having spots' and 'nose picking'.

6) The investigation has to be a <u>FAIR TEST</u> to make sure the evidence is <u>valid</u>...

*See page 2 for more on validity.*

## To Make an Investigation a Fair Test You Have to Control the Variables

1) In a lab experiment you usually <u>change one variable</u> and <u>measure</u> how it affects the <u>other variable</u>.

> EXAMPLE: you might change <u>only</u> the temperature of an enzyme-controlled reaction and measure how it affects the rate of reaction.

2) To make it a fair test <u>everything else</u> that could affect the results should <u>stay the same</u> (otherwise you can't tell if the thing you're changing is causing the results or not — the data won't be valid).

> EXAMPLE continued: you need to keep the pH the same, otherwise you won't know if any change in the rate of reaction is caused by the change in temperature, or the change in pH.

3) The variable you CHANGE is called the INDEPENDENT variable.

4) The variable you MEASURE is called the DEPENDENT variable.

5) The variables that you KEEP THE SAME are called CONTROL variables.

> EXAMPLE continued:
> Independent variable = temperature
> Dependent variable = rate of reaction
> Control variables = pH, volume of reactants, concentration of reactants etc.

6) To make sure no other factors are affecting the result, you can include a CONTROL EXPERIMENT — an experiment that's kept under the <u>same conditions</u> as the rest of the investigation, but doesn't have anything done to it.

> EXAMPLE continued: for each temperature investigated, you could set up an experiment with all of the reactants in the same volumes and concentrations, at the same pH, but include <u>no enzyme</u>. This would show that the result at each temperature is down to the action of the enzyme, and not any of the other things in the test tubes.

*The Scientific Process*

# Designing Investigations

## Trial Runs help Figure out the Range and Interval of Variable Values

1) It's a good idea to do a trial run (preliminary investigation) first — a quick version of the experiment.

2) Trial runs are used to figure out the range of variable values used in the proper experiment (the upper and lower limit). If you don't get a change in the dependent variable at the upper values in the trial run, you might narrow the range in the proper experiment. But if you still get a big change at the upper values you might increase the range.

3) And trial runs can be used to figure out the interval (gaps) between the values too. The intervals can't be too small (otherwise the experiment would take ages), or too big (otherwise you might miss something).

4) Trial runs can also help you figure out whether or not your experiment is repeatable. E.g. if you repeat it three times and the results are all similar, the experiment is repeatable.

**EXAMPLE continued:**

You might do a trial run with a range of 10-50 °C. If there was no reaction at the top end (e.g. 40-50 °C), you might narrow the range to 10-40 °C for the proper experiment.

If using 1 °C intervals doesn't give you much change in the rate of reaction each time you might decide to use 5 °C intervals, e.g. 10, 15, 20, 25, 30, 35 °C...

## It Can Be Hard to Control the Variables in a Study

It's important that a study is a fair test, just like a lab experiment. It's a lot trickier to control the variables in a study than in a lab experiment though (see previous page). Sometimes you can't control them all, but you can use a control group to help. This is a group of whatever you're studying (people, plants, lemmings, etc.) that's kept under the same conditions as the group in the experiment, but doesn't have anything done to it.

**EXAMPLE:** If you're studying the effect of pesticides on crop growth, pesticide is applied to one field but not to another field (the control field). Both fields are planted with the same crop, and are in the same area (so they get the same weather conditions). The control field is there to try and account for variables like the weather, which don't stay the same all the time, but could affect the results.

## Investigations Can be Hazardous

1) A hazard is something that can potentially cause harm. Hazards include:

- Microorganisms, e.g. some bacteria can make you ill.
- Chemicals, e.g. sulfuric acid can burn your skin and alcohols catch fire easily.
- Fire, e.g. an unattended Bunsen burner is a fire hazard.
- Electricity, e.g. faulty electrical equipment could give you a shock.

*Hmm... Where did my bacteria sample go?*

2) Scientists need to manage the risk of hazards by doing things to reduce them. For example:

- If you're working with sulfuric acid, always wear gloves and safety goggles. This will reduce the risk of the acid coming into contact with your skin and eyes.
- If you're using a Bunsen burner, stand it on a heat proof mat. This will reduce the risk of starting a fire.

*You can find out about potential hazards by looking in textbooks, doing some internet research, or asking your teacher.*

## You won't get a trial run at the exam, so get learnin'...

All this info needs to be firmly lodged in your memory. Learn the names of the different variables — if you remember that the variable you chaNge is called the iNdependent variable, you can figure out the other ones.

# Collecting Data

It's important to collect data that you can <u>trust</u> — data that's <u>repeatable</u>, <u>reproducible</u>, <u>accurate</u> and <u>precise</u>. Read on my intrepid friend...

## Data Should be as Accurate and Precise as Possible

1) To show that results are repeatable, and so improve validity, readings should be repeated at least <u>three times</u> and a <u>mean</u> (average) calculated.

2) To make sure that results are reproducible you can cross check them by taking a <u>second set of readings</u> with <u>another instrument</u> (or a <u>different observer</u>).

3) Checking that results match with <u>secondary sources</u>, e.g. other studies, also increases the validity.

4) Data also needs to be ACCURATE. Really accurate results are <u>really close</u> to the <u>true answer</u>. The accuracy of the results usually depends on the <u>method</u> and the <u>equipment</u> used, e.g. when measuring the <u>rate</u> of an enzyme-controlled reaction, you should use a <u>stopwatch</u> to aoourately measure the time.

5) Data also needs to be PRECISE. Precise results are ones where the data is <u>all really close</u> to the <u>mean</u> (i.e. not spread out).

*Remember — to be valid, data has to be repeatable and reproducible (p. 2).*

## The Equipment has to be Right for the Job

1) The measuring equipment used has to be <u>sensitive enough</u> to measure the changes being looked for. For example, if you need to measure changes of 1 ml you need to use a measuring cylinder that can measure in 1 ml steps — it'd be no good trying with one that only measures 10 ml steps.

2) The <u>smallest change</u> a measuring instrument can <u>detect</u> is called its RESOLUTION. E.g. some mass balances have a resolution of 1 g, some have a resolution of 0.1 g, and some are even more sensitive.

3) Also, equipment needs to be <u>calibrated</u> so that the data is <u>more accurate</u>. E.g. mass balances need to be set to zero before you start weighing things.

## You Need to Look out for Errors and Anomalous Results

1) The results of experiments will always <u>vary a bit</u> because of RANDOM ERRORS — tiny differences caused by things like <u>human errors</u> in <u>measuring</u>.

2) Their effect can be <u>reduced</u> by taking many readings and calculating the <u>mean</u>.

3) If the <u>same error</u> is made every time, it's called a SYSTEMATIC ERROR. For example, if you measured from the very end of your ruler instead of from the 0 cm mark every time, all your measurements would be a bit small.

4) Just to make things more complicated, if a systematic error is caused by using <u>equipment</u> that <u>isn't zeroed properly</u> it's called a ZERO ERROR. For example, if a mass balance always reads 1 gram before you put anything on it, all your measurements will be 1 gram too heavy.

5) Some systematic errors can be <u>compensated</u> for if you know about them though, e.g. if your mass balance always reads 1 gram before you put anything on it you can subtract 1 gram from all your results.

6) Sometimes you get a result that <u>doesn't seem to fit in</u> with the rest at all.

7) These results are called ANOMALOUS RESULTS.

8) They should be <u>investigated</u> to find out what <u>caused them</u>. If you can work out what happened (e.g. something was measured wrong) you can <u>ignore</u> them when processing the results.

*Repeating the experiment in the exact same way and calculating an average won't correct a systematic error.*

| Park | No. of pigeons | No. of zebras |
|------|----------------|---------------|
| A | 28 | 1 |
| B | 42 | 2 |
| C | 1127 | 0 |

## Zero error — sounds like a Bruce Willis film...

Weirdly, data can be really <u>precise</u> but <u>not very accurate</u>, e.g. a fancy piece of lab equipment might give results that are precise, but if it's not calibrated properly those results won't be accurate.

# Processing and Presenting Data

If you've got some results from an experiment, you might need to <u>process</u> and <u>present</u> them so you can look for <u>patterns</u> and <u>relationships</u> in them.

## Data Needs to be Organised

1) Tables are dead useful for <u>organising data</u>.

2) If you have to draw a table <u>use a ruler</u>, make sure <u>each column</u> has a <u>heading</u> (including the <u>units</u>) and keep it neat and tidy.

3) You might be asked to <u>describe</u> the results in a table or <u>pick out</u> an anomalous result.

4) But tables aren't always that great for showing <u>patterns</u> in data, so you might be asked to draw a <u>graph</u>.

## You Might Have to Process Some Data

1) The repeats of an experiment should be used to calculate a <u>mean</u> (average). To do this <u>ADD TOGETHER</u> all the data values and <u>DIVIDE</u> by the total number of values in the sample.

2) You might also need to calculate the <u>range</u> (how spread out the data is). To do this find the <u>LARGEST</u> number and <u>SUBTRACT</u> the <u>SMALLEST</u> number from it.

*Ignore anomalous results when calculating these.*

### EXAMPLE

| Test tube | Repeat 1 (g) | Repeat 2 (g) | Repeat 3 (g) | Mean (g) | Range (g) |
|-----------|--------------|--------------|--------------|----------|-----------|
| A | 28 | 37 | 32 | $(28 + 37 + 32) \div 3 = 32.3$ | $37 - 28 = 9$ |
| B | 47 | 51 | 60 | $(47 + 51 + 60) \div 3 = 52.7$ | $60 - 47 = 13$ |
| C | 68 | 72 | 70 | $(68 + 72 + 70) \div 3 = 70.0$ | $72 - 68 = 4$ |

## If the Data Comes in Categories, Present It in a Bar Chart

1) If either the independent or dependent variable is <u>categoric</u> (comes in distinct categories, e.g. blood types, metals) you should use a <u>bar chart</u> to display the data.

2) You also use them if one of the variables is <u>discrete</u> (the data can be counted in chunks, where there's no in-between value, e.g. number of people is discrete because you can't have half a person).

3) There are some <u>golden rules</u> you need to follow for <u>drawing</u> bar charts:

① Remember to include the <u>units</u>.

② <u>Label both axes</u>.

③ Leave a <u>gap between</u> different categories.

④ Draw it nice and <u>big</u> (covering at least half of the graph paper).

⑤ If you've got more than one set of data <u>include a key</u>.

**Ice Cream Sales in Froggartland and Broccoliland**

Number sold (thousands) — Ice cream flavour: Chocolate, Mint, Strawberry, Broccoli

Key: Froggartland, Broccoliland

## Discrete variables love bar charts — although they'd never tell anyone that...

The stuff on this page might all seem a bit basic, but it's <u>easy marks</u> in the exams (which you'll kick yourself if you don't get). Examiners are a bit picky when it comes to bar charts — if you don't draw them properly they won't be happy. Also, <u>double check</u> any mean or range <u>calculations</u> you do, just to be sure they're correct.

# Presenting Data

Scientists just <u>love</u> presenting data as <u>line graphs</u> (weirdos)...

## If the Data is Continuous, Plot a Line Graph

1) If the independent and the dependent variable are <u>continuous</u> (numerical data that can have any value within a range, e.g. length, volume, temperature) you should use a <u>line graph</u> to display the data.

2) Here are the <u>rules</u> for <u>drawing</u> line graphs:

**①** Remember to include the <u>units</u>.

**②** Put the <u>dependent</u> variable (the thing you measure) on the <u>y-axis</u> (the <u>vertical</u> one).

**③** <u>Label both axes</u>.

**④** If you've got more than one set of data <u>include a key</u>.

**⑤** Draw it nice and <u>big</u> (covering at least half of the graph paper).

**⑥** Put the <u>independent</u> variable (the thing you change) on the <u>x-axis</u> (the <u>horizontal</u> one).

*Graph to Show Rate of Enzyme-controlled Reaction Against Temperature* — Rate of reaction ($cm^3/s$) vs Temperature (°C). anomalous result

**⑧** To plot the points, use a <u>sharp pencil</u> and make a <u>neat little cross</u> (don't do blobs). nice clear mark / smudged / unclear marks

**⑦** <u>Don't join the dots up</u>. You need to draw a <u>line of best fit</u> (or a <u>curve of best fit</u> if your points make a curve). When drawing a line (or curve), try to draw the line <u>through</u> or as <u>near</u> to <u>as many points as possible</u>, ignoring anomalous results.

3) Line graphs are used to <u>show the relationship</u> between two variables (just like other graphs).

4) Data can show <u>three</u> different types of correlation (relationship):

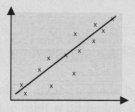

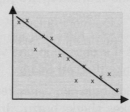

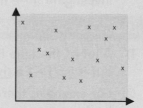

<u>POSITIVE</u> correlation — as one variable <u>increases</u> the other <u>increases</u>.

<u>NEGATIVE</u> correlation — as one variable <u>increases</u> the other <u>decreases</u>.

<u>NO</u> correlation — there's <u>no relationship</u> between the two variables.

5) You need to be able to describe the following relationships on line graphs too:

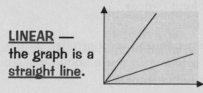

<u>LINEAR</u> — the graph is a <u>straight line</u>.

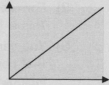

<u>DIRECTLY PROPORTIONAL</u> — the graph is a <u>straight line</u> which goes through the <u>origin</u> (0, 0), and both variables increase (or decrease) in the <u>same ratio</u>.

## There's a positive correlation between revision and boredom...

...but there's also a positive correlation between <u>revision</u> and getting a <u>better mark in an exam</u>. Cover the page and write down the <u>eight things</u> you need to remember when <u>drawing line graphs</u>. No sneaky peeking either — I saw you.

# Drawing Conclusions

Congratulations — you've made it to the fun part — <u>drawing conclusions</u>.

## You Can Only Conclude What the Data Shows and NO MORE

1) Drawing conclusions might seem pretty straightforward — you just <u>look at the data</u> and <u>say what pattern or relationship you see</u> between the dependent and independent variables.

EXAMPLE: The table on the right shows the heights of pea plant seedlings grown for three weeks with different fertilisers.

| Fertiliser | Mean growth / mm |
|------------|------------------|
| A | 13.5 |
| B | 19.5 |
| No fertiliser | 5.5 |

<u>CONCLUSION</u>: Fertiliser <u>B</u> makes <u>pea plant</u> seedlings grow taller over a <u>three week</u> period than fertiliser A.

2) But you've got to be really careful that your conclusion <u>matches the data</u> you've got and <u>doesn't go any further</u>.

EXAMPLE continued: You <u>CAN'T</u> conclude that fertiliser B makes <u>any other type of plant</u> grow taller than fertiliser A — the results could be totally different.

3) You also need to be able to <u>use the results</u> to <u>justify your conclusion</u> (i.e. back up your conclusion with some specific data).

EXAMPLE continued: Over the three week period, fertiliser B made the pea plants grow 6 mm more on average than fertiliser A.

## Correlation DOES NOT mean Cause

1) If two things are correlated (i.e. there's a relationship between them) it <u>doesn't</u> necessarily mean that a change in one variable is <u>causing</u> the change in the other — this is REALLY IMPORTANT, DON'T FORGET IT.

2) There are <u>three possible reasons</u> for a correlation:

### ① CHANCE

1) Even though it might seem a bit weird, it's possible that two things show a correlation in a study purely because of <u>chance</u>.

2) For example, one study might find a correlation between people's hair colour and how good they are at frisbee. But other scientists don't get a correlation when they investigate it — the results of the first study are just a fluke.

### ② LINKED BY A 3rd VARIABLE

1) A lot of the time it may <u>look</u> as if a change in one variable is causing a change in the other, but it <u>isn't</u> — a <u>third variable links</u> the two things.

2) For example, there's a correlation between water temperature and shark attacks. This obviously isn't because warmer water makes sharks crazy. Instead, they're linked by a third variable — the number of people swimming (more people swim when the water's hotter, and with more people in the water you get more shark attacks).

### ③ CAUSE

1) Sometimes a change in one variable does <u>cause</u> a change in the other.

2) For example, there's a correlation between smoking and lung cancer. This is because chemicals in tobacco smoke cause lung cancer.

3) You can only conclude that a correlation is due to cause when you've <u>controlled all the variables</u> that could, just could, be affecting the result. (For the smoking example above this would include things like age and exposure to other things that cause cancer).

## I conclude that this page is a bit dull...

...yup, I lied at the start. Although, just because I find it dull doesn't mean that I can conclude it's dull (you might think it's the most interesting thing since that kid got his head stuck in the railings). In an exam you could be given a <u>conclusion</u> and asked <u>whether the data supports it</u> — so make sure you understand this page.

# Planning and Evaluating Investigations

In an exam, you could be asked to <u>plan</u> or <u>describe</u> how you'd <u>carry out</u> an investigation. You might also be asked to say what you think of someone else's. Fear not, here's how you'd go about such things...

## You Need to Be Able to Plan a Good Experiment

Here are some <u>general tips</u> on what to include when planning an experiment:

1) Say <u>what</u> you're <u>measuring</u> (i.e. what the <u>dependent variable</u> will be).
2) Say <u>what</u> you're <u>changing</u> (i.e. what the <u>independent variable</u> will be) and describe <u>how</u> you'll change it.
3) Describe the <u>method</u> and the <u>apparatus</u> you'd use (e.g. to measure the variables).
4) Describe what <u>variables</u> you're keeping <u>constant</u> — and <u>how</u> you're going to do it.
5) Say that you need to <u>repeat</u> the experiment three times, to make sure the results are <u>repeatable</u>.
6) Say whether you're using a <u>control</u> or not.

Here's an <u>idea</u> of the sort of thing you might be asked in an exam and what you might write as an answer...

### Exam-style Question:

1   Describe an investigation to find out what effect temperature has on the rate of photosynthesis in Canadian pondweed.

### Example Answer:

Put a certain mass of Canadian pondweed and water in a test tube. Connect the tube to a capillary tube containing water and a syringe, then put it in a water bath at 10 °C near a source of white light.

Leave the experiment for a set amount of time. As the pondweed photosynthesises, the oxygen released will collect in the capillary tube. At the end of the experiment, use the syringe to draw the gas bubble in the tube up alongside a ruler and measure the length of the gas bubble. This is proportional to the volume of $O_2$ produced.

Repeat the experiment with the water bath at different temperatures (e.g. 20 °C, 30 °C, and 40 °C). Three repeats should be carried out at each temperature to make sure the results are repeatable. For each repeat: the pondweed should be left to photosynthesise for the same amount of time (measured with a stopwatch), the test tube should be the same distance away from the light source (measured with a ruler), and the same mass of pondweed should be used (measured with a balance).

A control should also be set up at each temperature. This should be a test tube containing water and boiled pondweed (so that it can't photosynthesise).

Use the results from the repeats to find an average rate of photosynthesis at each temperature.

## You Could Be Asked to Evaluate An Investigation

And finally — you might be asked to <u>evaluate</u> (assess) someone's investigation, data or conclusion. You need to think about the following things:

1) Method: Was it a <u>fair test</u>? Was the best method of <u>data collection</u> used?
2) Repeatability: Were enough <u>repeat measurements</u> taken? Were the repeated measurements <u>similar</u>?
3) Reproducibility: Are the results <u>comparable</u> to similar experiments done by <u>other people</u>?
4) Validity: Does the data <u>answer</u> the <u>original question</u>?

If the answer to <u>all</u> of these questions is a <u>firm</u> '<u>yes</u>', you can have a <u>good degree of confidence</u> in the data and conclusion. If the answer to <u>any</u> of them is '<u>no</u>' or '<u>umm, I don't know</u>', then you might want to reconsider the data and conclusion. Have a think about how the investigation could be <u>improved</u> to get <u>repeatable</u>, <u>reproducible</u> and <u>valid results</u>.

## Plan your way to exam success...

You might have to write a <u>long, extended answer</u> to any questions like this in an exam. Just remember to <u>think</u> about what you're going to say <u>beforehand</u> and in what order — that way you're <u>less likely</u> to <u>forget</u> something <u>important</u>. Like what it is you're actually measuring, or what the different variables are, say.

# Cells

All living things are made of <u>cells</u>. When someone first peered down a microscope at a slice of cork and drew the <u>boxes</u> they saw, little did they know that they'd seen the <u>building blocks</u> of <u>every organism on the planet</u>.

## Plant and Animal Cells have Similarities and Differences

Most <u>human cells</u>, like most <u>animal</u> cells, have the following parts — make sure you know them all:

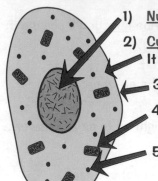

1) <u>Nucleus</u> — contains <u>genetic material</u> that controls the activities of the cell.

2) <u>Cytoplasm</u> — gel-like substance where most of the <u>chemical reactions</u> happen. It contains <u>enzymes</u> (see page 38) that control these chemical reactions.

3) <u>Cell membrane</u> — holds the cell together and controls what goes <u>in</u> and <u>out</u>.

4) <u>Mitochondria</u> — these are where most of the reactions for <u>respiration</u> take place (see page 29). Respiration releases <u>energy</u> that the cell needs to work.

5) <u>Ribosomes</u> — these are where <u>proteins</u> are made in the cell.

Plant cells usually have <u>all the bits</u> that <u>animal</u> cells have, plus a few <u>extra</u> things that animal cells <u>don't</u> have:

1) Rigid <u>cell wall</u> — made of <u>cellulose</u>. It <u>supports</u> the cell and strengthens it.

2) <u>Permanent vacuole</u> — contains <u>cell sap</u>, a weak solution of sugar and salts.

3) <u>Chloroplasts</u> — these absorb <u>light energy</u> during <u>photosynthesis</u>, which makes food for the plant (see page 58). They contain a <u>green</u> substance called <u>chlorophyll</u>.

The cells of algae (e.g. seaweed) also have a rigid cell wall and chloroplasts.

## Yeast is a Single-Celled Organism

Yeast is a <u>microorganism</u>. A yeast cell has a <u>nucleus</u>, <u>cytoplasm</u>, and a <u>cell membrane</u> surrounded by a <u>cell wall</u>.

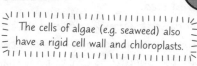
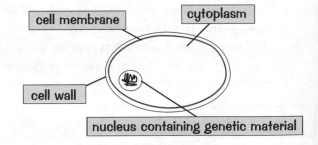

cell membrane

cytoplasm

cell wall

nucleus containing genetic material

## Bacterial Cells Have No Nucleus

Bacteria are also <u>single-celled</u> microorganisms.

1) A bacterial cell has <u>cytoplasm</u> and a <u>cell membrane</u> surrounded by a <u>cell wall</u>.

2) The <u>genetic material</u> floats in the cytoplasm because bacterial cells don't have a distinct <u>nucleus</u>. Some of the genes are found in circular structures called <u>plasmids</u>.

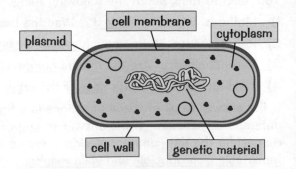

plasmid

cell membrane

cytoplasm

cell wall

genetic material

## There's quite a bit to learn in biology — but that's life, I guess...

On this page are <u>typical cells</u> with all the typical bits you need to know. But cells <u>aren't</u> all the same — they have different <u>structures</u> and <u>produce</u> different substances depending on the <u>job</u> they do. And that's up next...

# Specialised Cells

The last page shows the structure of some typical cells. However, most cells are specialised for their specific function, so their structure can vary...

## 1) Palisade Leaf Cells Are Adapted for Photosynthesis

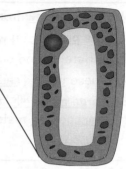

1) Packed with chloroplasts for photosynthesis. More of them are crammed at the top of the cell — so they're nearer the light.

2) Tall shape means a lot of surface area exposed down the side for absorbing $CO_2$ from the air in the leaf.

3) Thin shape means that you can pack loads of them in at the top of a leaf.

Palisade leaf cells are grouped together at the top of the leaf where most of the photosynthesis happens.

## 2) Guard Cells Are Adapted to Open and Close Pores

guard cell

stoma
(plural — stomata)

1) Special kidney shape which opens and closes the stomata (pores) in a leaf.

2) When the plant has lots of water the guard cells fill with it and go plump and turgid (p. 17). This makes the stomata open so gases can be exchanged for photosynthesis.

3) When the plant is short of water, the guard cells lose water and become flaccid (p. 17), making the stomata close. This helps stop too much water vapour escaping.

4) Thin outer walls and thickened inner walls make the opening and closing work.

5) They're also sensitive to light and close at night to save water without losing out on photosynthesis.

6) You usually find more stomata on the undersides of leaves than on the top. The lower surface is shaded and cooler — so less water is lost through the stomata than if they were on the upper surface.

Guard cells are therefore adapted for gas exchange and controlling water loss within a leaf.

## 3) Red Blood Cells Are Adapted to Carry Oxygen

1) Concave shape gives a big surface area for absorbing oxygen. It also helps them pass smoothly inside capillaries to reach body cells.

2) They're packed with haemoglobin — the pigment that absorbs the oxygen.

3) They have no nucleus, to leave even more room for haemoglobin.

Red blood cells are an important part of the blood.

## 4) Sperm and Egg Cells Are Specialised for Reproduction

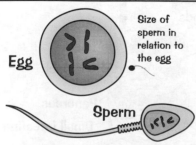

Egg

Size of sperm in relation to the egg

Sperm

1) The main functions of an egg cell are to carry the female DNA and to nourish the developing embryo in the early stages. The egg cell contains huge food reserves to feed the embryo.

2) When a sperm fuses with the egg, the egg's membrane instantly changes its structure to stop any more sperm getting in. This makes sure the offspring end up with the right amount of DNA.

3) The function of a sperm is basically to get the male DNA to the female DNA. It has a long tail and a streamlined head to help it swim to the egg. There are a lot of mitochondria in the cell to provide the energy needed.

4) Sperm also carry enzymes in their heads to digest through the egg cell membrane. Sperm and eggs are very important cells in reproduction.

## Beans, flying saucers, tadpoles — cells are masters of disguise...

These cells all have all the bits shown on the last page, even though they look completely different and do totally different jobs. Apart from red blood cells that is, which are a bit special, e.g. they don't have a nucleus.

# Tissues, Organs and Organ Systems

How, you might wonder, does having all these <u>specialised cells</u> mean you end up with a working <u>human</u> or <u>squirrel</u>... the answer's <u>organisation</u>.  Otherwise you'd just have a meaty splodge.

## Large Multicellular Organisms are Made Up of Organ Systems

1) As you know from the previous page, <u>specialised cells</u> carry out a <u>particular function</u>.
2) The <u>process</u> by which cells become specialised for a particular job is called <u>differentiation</u>.
3) Differentiation occurs during the <u>development</u> of a multicellular organism.
4) These <u>specialised cells</u> form <u>tissues</u>, which form <u>organs</u>, which form <u>organ systems</u> (see below).
5) <u>Large multicellular organisms</u> (e.g. squirrels) have different <u>systems</u> inside them for <u>exchanging</u> and <u>transporting</u> materials.

## Similar Cells are Organised into Tissues

A <u>tissue</u> is a <u>group</u> of <u>similar cells</u> that work together to carry out a particular <u>function</u>.
It can include <u>more than one type</u> of cell.  In <u>mammals</u> (like humans),
examples of tissues include:

1) <u>Muscular tissue</u>, which <u>contracts</u> (shortens) to <u>move</u> whatever it's attached to.
2) <u>Glandular tissue</u>, which <u>makes</u> and <u>secretes</u> chemicals like <u>enzymes</u> and <u>hormones</u>.
3) <u>Epithelial tissue</u>, which <u>covers</u> some parts of the body, e.g. the <u>inside</u> of the <u>gut</u>.

**Epithelial cell**

less than
0.1 mm

**Epithelial tissue**

## Tissues are Organised into Organs

An <u>organ</u> is a group of <u>different tissues</u> that work together to perform a
certain <u>function</u>.  For example, the <u>stomach</u> is an organ made of these tissues:

1) <u>Muscular tissue</u>, which allows food to <u>move through</u> the <u>digestive system</u>.
2) <u>Glandular tissue</u>, which makes <u>digestive juices</u> to digest food.
3) <u>Epithelial tissue</u>, which covers the <u>outside</u> and <u>inside</u> of the stomach.

**Stomach**

about 10 cm
(over 1000 times
longer than an
epithelial cell)

## Organs are Organised into Organ Systems

An <u>organ system</u> is a <u>group of organs</u> working together to perform a particular
<u>function</u>.  For example, the <u>digestive system</u> (found in humans and mammals)
<u>breaks down food</u> and is made up of these organs:

1) <u>Glands</u> (e.g. the <u>pancreas</u> and <u>salivary glands</u>),
   which produce <u>digestive juices</u>.
2) The <u>stomach</u> and <u>small intestine</u>, which <u>digest</u> food.
3) The <u>liver</u>, which produces <u>bile</u>.
4) The <u>small intestine</u>, which <u>absorbs</u> soluble <u>food</u> molecules.
5) The <u>large intestine</u>, which <u>absorbs water</u> from undigested food,
   leaving <u>faeces</u>.

The digestive system <u>exchanges materials</u> with the <u>environment</u>
by <u>taking in nutrients</u> (i.e. food) and <u>releasing substances</u> such as bile.
There's more on the digestive system on pages 39-40.

**Salivary glands**

**Liver**

**Digestive system**

Stomach

Pancreas

Small intestine

Large intestine

You need to know where these organs
are on a diagram — see page 40.

## Soft and quilted — the best kind of tissues...

OK, <u>cells</u> are organised into <u>tissues</u>, the tissues into <u>organs</u>, and the organs into a whole <u>organism</u>.  Or, to put it
another way, an <u>organism</u> consists of <u>organs</u> which are made of <u>tissues</u> which are groups of <u>cells</u> working together.

# Plant Tissues and Organs

It's not just animals that are organised — plants also keep their specialised cells neat and tidy.

## Plant Cells Are Organised Into Tissues And Organs Too

Plants are made of organs like stems, roots and leaves. These organs are made of tissues. Examples of plant tissues are:

For more on photosynthesis, see page 58.

1) Epidermal tissue — this covers the whole plant.

2) Palisade mesophyll tissue — this is the part of the leaf where most photosynthesis happens.

3) Spongy mesophyll tissue — this is also in the leaf, and contains big air spaces to allow gases to diffuse in and out of cells.

4) Xylem and phloem — they transport things like water, mineral ions and sucrose around the plant (through the roots, stems and leaves — see page 63 for more).

## The Leaf Contains Epidermal, Mesophyll, Xylem and Phloem Tissue

You need to know the internal structure of a leaf:

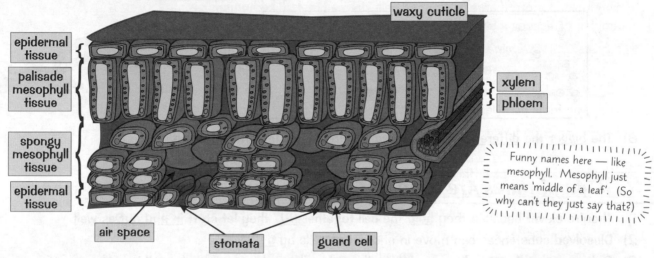

waxy cuticle

epidermal tissue

palisade mesophyll tissue

spongy mesophyll tissue

epidermal tissue

xylem

phloem

air space

stomata

guard cell

Funny names here — like mesophyll. Mesophyll just means 'middle of a leaf'. (So why can't they just say that?)

## The Xylem and Phloem are in Different Places in Roots and Stems

The xylem and phloem usually run alongside each other. Where they're found in each type of plant structure is related to the xylem's other function — support.

You need to learn these two examples:

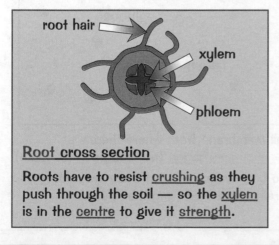

root hair

xylem

phloem

**Root cross section**

Roots have to resist crushing as they push through the soil — so the xylem is in the centre to give it strength.

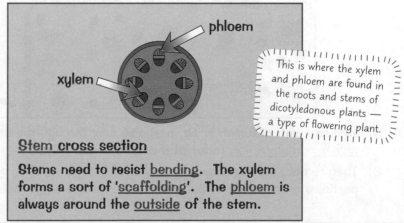

phloem

xylem

This is where the xylem and phloem are found in the roots and stems of dicotyledonous plants — a type of flowering plant.

**Stem cross section**

Stems need to resist bending. The xylem forms a sort of 'scaffolding'. The phloem is always around the outside of the stem.

## Don't let revision stress you out — just go with the phloem...

In the exam, you might have to label a diagram to show where the different types of specialised tissue are found in a plant. Make sure you know what they do too — and no, it's not just sitting round looking pretty.

# Diffusion

Particles <u>move about randomly</u>, and after a bit they end up <u>evenly spaced</u>.  It's not rocket science, is it...

## Don't Be Put Off by the Fancy Word

1) "<u>Diffusion</u>" is simple.  It's just the <u>gradual movement</u> of particles from places where there are <u>lots</u> of them to places where there are <u>fewer</u> of them.

2) That's all it is — just the <u>natural tendency</u> for stuff to <u>spread out</u>.

3) Unfortunately you also have to learn the fancy way of saying the same thing, which is this:

> ### <u>DIFFUSION</u> is the <u>spreading out</u> of <u>particles</u> from an area of <u>HIGH CONCENTRATION</u> to an area of <u>LOW CONCENTRATION</u>

4) Diffusion happens in both <u>solutions</u> and <u>gases</u> — that's because the particles in these substances are free to <u>move about</u> randomly.

5) The <u>simplest type</u> is when different <u>gases</u> diffuse through each other.
This is what's happening when the smell of perfume (or a skunk) diffuses through the air in a room:

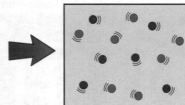 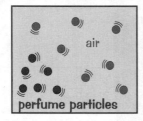

perfume
particles
diffused
in the air

6) The <u>bigger</u> the <u>difference</u> in concentration, the <u>faster</u> the diffusion rate.

## Cell Membranes Are Kind of Clever...

1) They're clever because they <u>hold</u> the cell together <u>BUT</u> they let stuff <u>in and out</u> as well.

2) Dissolved substances can move in and out of cells by <u>diffusion</u>.

3) Only very <u>small</u> molecules can <u>diffuse</u> through cell membranes though — things like <u>oxygen</u> (needed for respiration — see page 29), <u>glucose</u>, <u>amino acids</u> and <u>water</u>.

4) <u>Big</u> molecules like <u>starch</u> and <u>proteins</u> can't fit through the membrane:

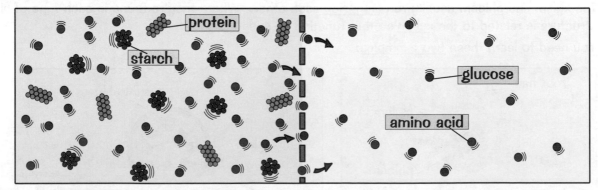

5) Just like with diffusion in air, particles flow through the cell membrane from where there's a <u>higher concentration</u> (a lot of them) to where there's a <u>lower concentration</u> (not such a lot of them).

6) They're only moving about <u>randomly</u> of course, so they go <u>both</u> ways — but if there are a lot <u>more</u> particles on one side of the membrane, there's a <u>net</u> (overall) movement <u>from</u> that side.

## Revision by diffusion — you wish...

Wouldn't that be great — if all the ideas in this book would just gradually drift across into your mind, from an area of <u>high concentration</u> (in the book) to an area of <u>low concentration</u> (in your mind — no offence). Actually, that probably will happen if you read it again.  Why don't you give it a go...

# *Osmosis*

If you've got your head round <u>diffusion</u>, osmosis will be a <u>breeze</u>. If not, have another look at the last page.

## Osmosis is a Special Case of Diffusion, That's All

<u>OSMOSIS</u> is the <u>movement of water molecules</u> across a <u>partially permeable membrane</u> from a region of <u>high water concentration</u> to a region of <u>low water concentration</u>.

1) A <u>partially permeable</u> membrane is just one with very small holes in it. So small, in fact, only tiny <u>molecules</u> (like water) can pass through them, and bigger molecules (e.g. <u>sucrose</u>) can't.

2) The water molecules actually pass <u>both ways</u> because water molecules <u>move about randomly</u> all the time.

3) But because there are <u>more</u> water molecules on one side than on the other, there's a steady <u>net flow</u> of water into the region with <u>fewer</u> water molecules, i.e. into the <u>stronger</u> sugar solution.

4) This means the <u>strong sugar</u> solution gets more <u>dilute</u> — the water acts like it's trying to "<u>even up</u>" the concentration.

5) But the wording can be confusing — an area of <u>high water concentration</u> is called a <u>dilute solution</u>. So osmosis can be described as the <u>movement of water</u> from a <u>dilute</u> to a <u>more concentrated solution</u>.

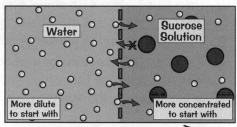

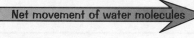

Net movement of water molecules

## Water Moves Into and Out of Cells by Osmosis

1) <u>Tissue fluid</u> surrounds the cells in the body — it's basically just <u>water</u> with <u>oxygen</u>, <u>glucose</u> and stuff dissolved in it. It's squeezed out of the <u>blood capillaries</u> to supply the cells with everything they need.

2) The tissue fluid will usually have a <u>different water concentration</u> to the fluid <u>inside</u> a cell — so <u>water</u> will either <u>move into</u> or <u>out of</u> the cell by <u>osmosis</u>:

| Water concentration in the tissue fluid | Tissue fluid is called... | Water moves? |
|---|---|---|
| <u>HIGHER</u> than in the cell fluid | a <u>HYPOTONIC</u> solution | <u>INTO</u> the cell |
| <u>LOWER</u> than in the cell fluid | a <u>HYPERTONIC</u> solution | <u>OUT OF</u> the cell |
| the <u>SAME</u> as in the cell fluid | an <u>ISOTONIC</u> solution | <u>NO NET</u> movement |

*You need to know what the terms hypotonic, hypertonic, isotonic, turgor and plasmolysis mean.*

## Turgor Pressure Supports Plant Tissues

Water moves in and out of <u>plant cells</u> and <u>tissues</u> by osmosis too.

1) When a plant is well watered, its cells draw water in by <u>osmosis</u> and become swollen — they're said to be <u>turgid</u>.

2) The contents of the cell push against the <u>inelastic cell wall</u>. This is called <u>turgor pressure</u> and it helps to <u>support</u> the plant tissues.

3) If a plant doesn't get <u>enough</u> water, its cells <u>lose</u> their turgor pressure — they become <u>flaccid</u>. The plant starts to <u>wilt</u> (droop).

4) If the plant's <u>really short</u> of water (like in a drought) the <u>cytoplasm</u> inside its cells starts to <u>shrink</u> and the membrane <u>pulls away</u> from the cell wall. This is called <u>plasmolysis</u> and the cell is said to be <u>plasmolysed</u>. The plant doesn't totally lose its shape though, because the <u>inelastic cell wall</u> keeps things in position.

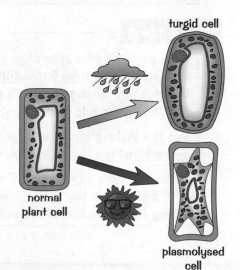

turgid cell

normal plant cell

plasmolysed cell

## *Osmosis — just a watered down version of diffusion*

Some tricky terms to remember here — try covering them up and writing down what they mean 'til you've got it.

# Diffusion and Osmosis Experiments

For all you non-believers — here are a few <u>experiments</u> you can do to see <u>diffusion</u> and <u>osmosis</u> in action.

## You Can Investigate Diffusion Using Agar Jelly

<u>Phenolphthalein</u> is a <u>pH indicator</u> — it's <u>pink</u> in alkaline solutions and <u>colourless</u> in acidic solutions.
You can use it to investigate <u>diffusion</u> in <u>agar jelly</u>:

1) First, make up some agar jelly with <u>phenolphthalein</u> and dilute <u>sodium hydroxide</u>. This will make the jelly a lovely shade of <u>pink</u>.

2) Then fill a <u>beaker</u> with some dilute <u>hydrochloric acid</u>. Using a <u>scalpel</u>, cut out a few <u>cubes</u> from the jelly and put them in the beaker of acid.

3) If you <u>leave</u> the cubes for a while they'll eventually turn <u>colourless</u> as the <u>acid diffuses into</u> the agar jelly and <u>neutralises</u> the sodium hydroxide.

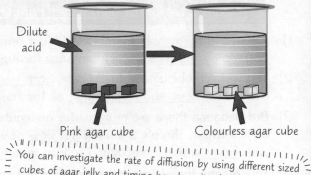

Dilute acid

Pink agar cube        Colourless agar cube

*You can investigate the rate of diffusion by using different sized cubes of agar jelly and timing how long it takes for each cube to go colourless. The cube with the largest surface area to volume ratio (see page 20) will lose its colour quickest.*

## You Can Investigate Osmosis Experimentally Too

### Potato cylinders

There's a fairly dull <u>experiment</u> you can do to show osmosis at work.

You cut up an innocent <u>potato</u> into identical cylinders, and get some beakers with <u>different sugar solutions</u> in them. One should be <u>pure water</u>, another should be a <u>very concentrated sugar solution</u>. Then you can have a few others with concentrations <u>in between</u>.

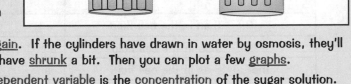

Pure water (hypotonic)        Potato cylinders        Rich sugar solution (hypertonic)

You measure the <u>length</u> of the cylinders, then leave a few cylinders in each beaker for half an hour or so.
Then you take them out and measure their lengths <u>again</u>. If the cylinders have drawn in water by osmosis, they'll be a bit <u>longer</u>. If water has been drawn out, they'll have <u>shrunk</u> a bit. Then you can plot a few <u>graphs</u>.

The <u>dependent variable</u> is the <u>chip length</u> and the <u>independent variable</u> is the <u>concentration</u> of the sugar solution. All <u>other</u> variables (volume of solution, temperature, time, type of sugar used, etc. etc.) must be kept the <u>same</u> in each case or the experiment won't be a <u>fair test</u>. You could measure <u>chip mass</u> instead of length — same idea.

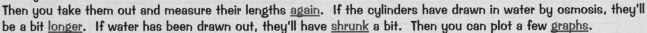

### Visking tubing

Tie a piece of wire around <u>one end</u> of some <u>Visking tubing</u> and put a <u>glass tube</u> in the <u>other end</u> — fix the tubing around it with wire. Then <u>pour</u> some sugar solution (hypertonic) down the glass tube into the Visking tubing.

Put the Visking tubing in a <u>beaker</u> of pure water (hypotonic) — <u>measure</u> where the sugar solution comes up to on the <u>glass tube</u>.

Leave the tubing <u>overnight</u>, then <u>measure</u> where the liquid is in the glass tube. <u>Water</u> should be <u>drawn into</u> the Visking tubing by osmosis and this will <u>force</u> the liquid <u>up</u> the glass tube.

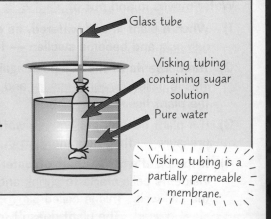

Glass tube

Visking tubing containing sugar solution

Pure water

*Visking tubing is a partially permeable membrane.*

## And to all you cold-hearted potato murderers...

And that's why it's bad to drink sea-water. The high <u>salt</u> content means you end up with a much <u>lower water concentration</u> in your blood and tissue fluid than in your cells. All the water is sucked out of your cells by osmosis and they <u>shrivel and die</u>. So next time you're stranded at sea, remember this page...

# Active Transport

Sometimes substances need to be absorbed against a concentration gradient, i.e. from a lower to a higher concentration. This process is lovingly referred to as ACTIVE TRANSPORT.

## Root Hairs are Specialised for Absorbing Water and Minerals

**Root Hair cell**

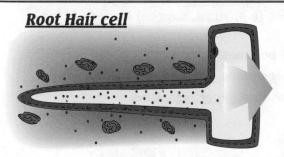

1) The cells on the surface of plant roots grow into long "hairs" which stick out into the soil.
2) This gives the plant a big surface area for absorbing water and mineral ions from the soil.
3) Most of the water and mineral ions that get into a plant are absorbed by the root hair cells.

## Root Hairs Take in Minerals Using Active Transport

1) The concentration of minerals is usually higher in the root hair cell than in the soil around it.
2) So normal diffusion doesn't explain how minerals are taken up into the root hair cell.
3) They should go the other way if they followed the rules of diffusion.
4) The answer is that a conveniently mysterious process called "active transport" is responsible.
5) Active transport allows the plant to absorb minerals from a very dilute solution, against a concentration gradient. This is essential for its growth. But active transport needs ENERGY from respiration to make it work.
6) Active transport also happens in humans, for example in taking glucose (sugar) from low concentrations in the intestines (see below), and from low concentrations in the kidney tubules.

## We Need Active Transport to Stop Us Starving

Active transport is used in the gut when there is a low concentration of nutrients in the gut, but a high concentration of nutrients in the blood.

1) When there's a higher concentration of glucose and amino acids in the gut they diffuse naturally into the blood.
2) BUT — sometimes there's a lower concentration of nutrients in the gut than there is in the blood.
3) This means that the concentration gradient is the wrong way.
4) The same process used in plant roots is used here....
   ..."Active transport".
5) Active transport allows nutrients to be taken into the blood, despite the fact that the concentration gradient is the wrong way.

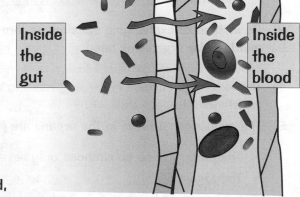

Inside the gut

Inside the blood

## Active transport sucks...

An important difference between active transport and diffusion is that active transport uses energy. Imagine a pen of sheep in a field. If you open the pen, the sheep will happily diffuse from the area of high sheep concentration into the field, which has a low sheep concentration — you won't have to do a thing. To get them back in the pen though, you'll have to put in quite a bit of energy.

# Gas and Solute Exchange

Substances might move by diffusion, osmosis and active transport, but that's not much use if they don't get to where they're needed.  This page is all about getting the <u>right stuff</u> to the <u>right place</u>, and <u>quickly enough</u>.

## Single-Celled Organisms have a High Surface Area : Volume Ratio

1) An organism needs to <u>supply</u> all its <u>cells</u> with the substances (e.g. sugar, oxygen) it needs to live (e.g. for processes like respiration and photosynthesis).

2) It also needs to <u>get rid of waste products</u> so it doesn't get poisoned.

3) How <u>easy</u> the exchange of substances is depends on the organism's <u>surface area to volume ratio</u>.

4) <u>Smaller</u> organisms have <u>bigger</u> surface area to volume ratios than <u>larger</u> organisms.

This can be a bit <u>tricky</u> to get your head around, but it's easier if you think of organisms as <u>cubes</u> for now.

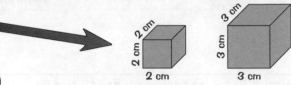

The <u>rate</u> of diffusion, osmosis and active transport is <u>higher</u> in organisms (or cubes) with a <u>larger surface area to volume ratio</u>.

The <u>smaller</u> cube has a <u>larger</u> surface area to volume ratio — this means <u>substances</u> would <u>move</u> into and out of this cube <u>faster</u>.

| Surface area (cm²) | 2 x 2 x 6 = 24 | 3 x 3 x 6 = 54 |
|---|---|---|
| Volume (cm³) | 2 x 2 x 2 = 8 | 3 x 3 x 3 = 27 |
| Surface area to volume ratio | 24 : 8 = <u>3 : 1</u> | 54 : 27 = <u>2 : 1</u> |

5) <u>Single-celled</u> organisms exchange substances differently to <u>multicellular</u> organisms (see below).

6) As they're only one cell big, substances can <u>diffuse straight into</u> and <u>out of</u> single-celled organisms <u>across</u> the <u>cell membrane</u>.  Diffusion is <u>quite quick</u> because:

- substances only have to <u>travel</u> a <u>short distance</u>,
- single-celled organisms have a <u>relatively large</u> surface area to volume ratio.

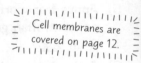
Cell membranes are covered on page 12.

## Multicellular Organisms Exchange Materials in Specialised Organs

1) <u>Exchanging substances</u> gets <u>trickier</u> in <u>bigger</u> and <u>more complex</u> organisms.

2) Diffusion across the outer membrane is <u>too slow</u> because:

- Some cells are <u>deep inside</u> the body — it's a <u>long way</u> from them to the <u>outside environment</u>.
- <u>Larger animals</u> have a <u>low surface area to volume ratio</u> — it's difficult to exchange enough substances to <u>supply</u> a <u>large volume of animal</u> through a relatively <u>small outer surface</u>.

3) So instead of exchanging substances through their outer membrane, multicellular organisms need <u>specialised exchange organs</u>, each with a <u>specialised exchange surface</u>.

$O_2$   $CO_2$

4) The exchange surface <u>structures</u> need to allow <u>enough</u> of the necessary substances to <u>pass through</u>.

5) The exchange surfaces in the organs are <u>ADAPTED</u> to maximise effectiveness:

- They are <u>thin</u>, so substances only have a <u>short distance</u> to <u>diffuse</u>.
- They have a <u>large surface area</u>, so <u>lots</u> of a substance can <u>diffuse</u> at once.
- Exchange surfaces in <u>animals</u> have <u>lots of blood vessels</u>, to get stuff into and out of the blood quickly.
- <u>Gas exchange surfaces</u> in animals (e.g. alveoli, page 21) are often <u>ventilated</u> too — air moves in and out.

## If you're bored, work out the surface area to volume ratio of a loved one...

Well I for one am relieved that I don't have to sit in a bath of beans every time I want a bite to eat.  And all because of our clever <u>internal exchange organs</u>.  Read on to see just how clever they are...

# Exchanging Materials in Mammals

This page is about how two different parts of mammals (including humans) are <u>adapted</u> so that gases and solutes can <u>diffuse</u> through them most <u>effectively</u>. The first bit is about how gases in the <u>lungs</u> get into and out of the blood. The second is about how digested food gets from the <u>gut</u> to the blood.

## Gas Exchange Happens in the Lungs

1) The job of the lungs is to transfer <u>oxygen</u> to the <u>blood</u> and to remove <u>waste carbon dioxide</u> from it.

2) To do this the lungs contain millions of little air sacs called <u>alveoli</u> where <u>gas exchange</u> takes place.

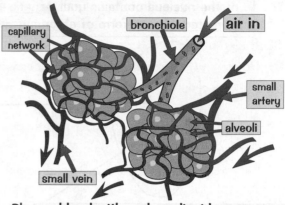

Blue = blood with carbon dioxide.
Red = blood with oxygen.

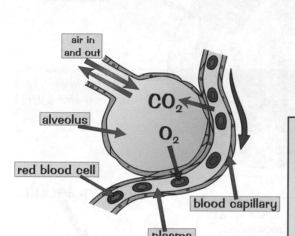

3) The alveoli are specialised to maximise the <u>diffusion</u> of oxygen and $CO_2$. They have:

- An <u>enormous</u> surface area (about 75 m² in humans).
- A <u>moist lining</u> for dissolving gases.
- Very <u>thin walls</u>.
- A <u>good blood supply</u>.

## The Villi Provide a Really Really Big Surface Area

1) The inside of the <u>small intestine</u> is covered in millions and millions of these tiny little projections called <u>villi</u>.

2) They increase the surface area in a big way so that digested food is <u>absorbed</u> much more quickly into the <u>blood</u>.

3) Notice they have

- a <u>single</u> layer of surface cells
- a very good <u>blood supply</u> to assist <u>quick absorption</u>.

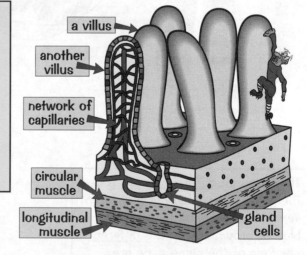

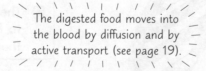

The digested food moves into the blood by diffusion and by active transport (see page 19).

## Al Veoli — the Italian gas man...

Living organisms are really <u>well adapted</u> for getting the substances they need to their cells — if they couldn't do this well, they'd <u>die out</u>. You might think I'm harping on about it but a <u>large surface area</u> is dead important in making exchange surfaces more effective — molecules can only diffuse through a membrane when they're right next to it, and a large surface area means <u>loads more molecules</u> are close to the membrane. If you're asked in an exam how something's adapted for a job, think about whether surface area is important — 'cos it often is.

# Genes and Chromosomes

This page is a bit tricky, but it's dead important you get to grips with all the stuff on it
— because you're going to hear more about it over the next few pages...

1) Most cells in your body have a <u>nucleus</u>.
The nucleus contains your <u>genetic</u>
<u>material</u> in the form of <u>chromosomes</u>.

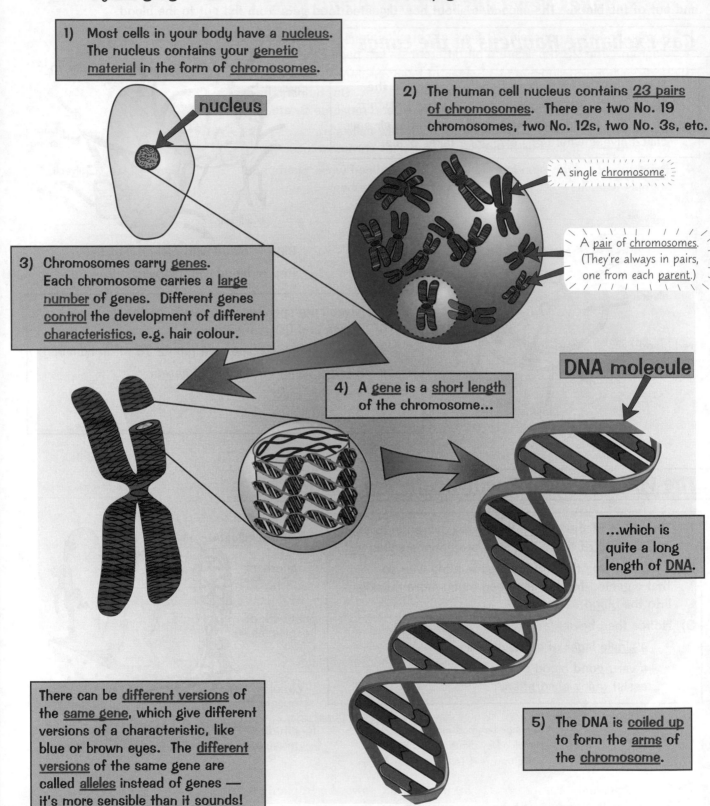

**nucleus**

2) The human cell nucleus contains <u>23 pairs</u>
<u>of chromosomes</u>. There are two No. 19
chromosomes, two No. 12s, two No. 3s, etc.

A single <u>chromosome</u>.

A <u>pair</u> of <u>chromosomes</u>.
(They're always in pairs,
one from each <u>parent</u>.)

3) Chromosomes carry <u>genes</u>.
Each chromosome carries a <u>large</u>
<u>number</u> of genes. Different genes
<u>control</u> the development of different
<u>characteristics</u>, e.g. hair colour.

4) A <u>gene</u> is a <u>short length</u>
of the chromosome...

**DNA molecule**

...which is
quite a long
length of <u>DNA</u>.

There can be <u>different versions</u> of
the <u>same gene</u>, which give different
versions of a characteristic, like
blue or brown eyes. The <u>different</u>
<u>versions</u> of the same gene are
called <u>alleles</u> instead of genes —
it's more sensible than it sounds!

5) The DNA is <u>coiled up</u>
to form the <u>arms</u> of
the <u>chromosome</u>.

## It's hard being a DNA molecule, there's so much to remember...

This is the bare bones of genetics, so you definitely need to understand <u>everything</u> on this page or you'll find
anything else about genetics quite hard. The best way to get all of these important facts engraved in your
mind is to <u>cover</u> the page, <u>scribble</u> down the main points and <u>sketch</u> out the diagrams...

# Cell Division — Mitosis

In order to <u>survive</u> and <u>grow</u>, our cells have got to be able to <u>divide</u>. And that means our <u>DNA</u> as well...

## Mitosis Makes New Cells for Growth and Repair

1) <u>Human body cells</u> contain <u>23 pairs of chromosomes</u> — as shown in the diagram. The 23rd pair are a bit different — see page 69.

2) <u>Body cells</u> normally have <u>two copies</u> of each <u>chromosome</u> — one from the organism's '<u>mother</u>', and one from its '<u>father</u>'. So, humans have two copies of chromosome 1, two copies of chromosome 2, etc.

3) When a body cell <u>divides</u> it needs to make new cells <u>identical</u> to the <u>original</u> cell — with the <u>same number</u> of chromosomes.

4) This type of cell division is called <u>mitosis</u>. It's used when plants and animals want to <u>grow</u> or to <u>replace</u> cells that have been <u>damaged</u>.

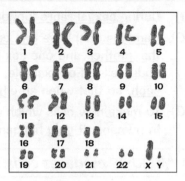

<u>"MITOSIS is when a cell reproduces itself by <u>splitting</u> to form <u>two identical offspring</u>."</u>

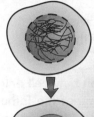

In a cell that's not dividing, the DNA is all spread out in <u>long strings</u>.

If the cell gets a signal to <u>divide</u>, it needs to <u>duplicate</u> its DNA — so there's one copy for each new cell. The DNA is copied and forms <u>X-shaped</u> chromosomes. Each 'arm' of the chromosome is an <u>exact duplicate</u> of the other.

The left arm has the same DNA as the right arm of the chromosome.

The chromosomes then <u>line up</u> at the centre of the cell and <u>cell fibres</u> pull them apart. The <u>two arms</u> of each chromosome go to <u>opposite ends</u> of the cell.

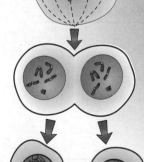

<u>Membranes</u> form around each of the sets of chromosomes. These become the <u>nuclei</u> of the two new cells.

Lastly, the <u>cytoplasm</u> divides.

You now have <u>two new cells</u> containing exactly the same DNA — they're <u>identical</u>.

Some organisms also <u>reproduce</u> by mitosis, e.g. strawberry plants form runners in this way, which become new plants. This is an example of <u>asexual</u> reproduction — see page 75.

## A cell's favourite computer game — divide and conquer...

This can seem tricky at first. But <u>don't worry</u> — just go through it <u>slowly</u>, one step at a time. This type of division produces <u>identical cells</u>, but there's another type which doesn't... (see next page)

# Cell Division — Meiosis

You thought mitosis was exciting. Hah. You ain't seen nothing yet...

## Meiosis Involves Two Divisions

1) During <u>sexual reproduction</u>, two cells called <u>gametes</u> (sex cells) <u>combine</u> to form a new individual.

2) <u>Gametes</u> only have <u>one copy</u> of each <u>chromosome</u>. This is so that you can combine one sex cell from the 'mother' and one sex cell from the 'father' and <u>still</u> end up with the <u>right number of chromosomes</u> in body cells. For example, human body cells have <u>46 chromosomes</u>. The <u>gametes</u> have <u>23 chromosomes</u> <u>each</u>, so that when an egg and sperm combine, you get 46 chromosomes again.

3) To make new cells which only have <u>half</u> the original number of chromosomes, cells divide by <u>meiosis</u>. In humans, it <u>only</u> happens in the <u>reproductive organs</u> (e.g. ovaries in females and testes in males).

*"<u>MEIOSIS</u> produces cells which have <u>half</u> the normal number of chromosomes."*

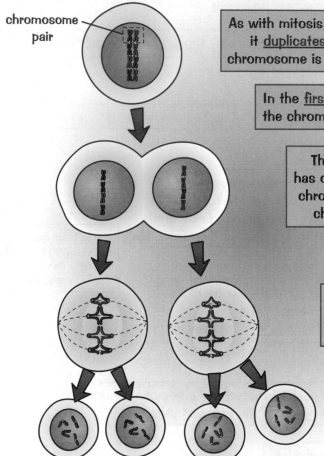

chromosome pair

As with mitosis, before the cell starts to divide, it <u>duplicates</u> its <u>DNA</u> — one arm of each chromosome is an <u>exact copy</u> of the other arm.

In the <u>first division</u> in meiosis (there are two divisions) the chromosome pairs <u>line up</u> in the centre of the cell.

The pairs are then <u>pulled apart</u>, so each new cell only has one copy of each chromosome. <u>Some</u> of the father's chromosomes (shown in blue) and <u>some</u> of the mother's chromosomes (shown in red) go into each new cell.

In the <u>second division</u> the chromosomes <u>line up</u> again in the centre of the cell. It's a lot like mitosis. The arms of the chromosomes are <u>pulled apart</u>.

You get four gametes each with only a <u>single set</u> of chromosomes in it.

## Two Gametes Join at Fertilisation to Produce a Single Body Cell

1) After the <u>gametes fuse</u> at <u>fertilisation</u>, the new cell has a <u>mixture</u> of two sets of chromosomes. This means the organism inherits genes (and therefore features) from <u>both</u> parents. This is how <u>sexual</u> reproduction produces <u>variation</u> (see p. 75).

2) The new cell <u>divides repeatedly</u> by <u>mitosis</u> to form <u>many cells</u>.

3) As the organism develops, these cells <u>differentiate</u> to form different kinds of <u>specialised cells</u>.

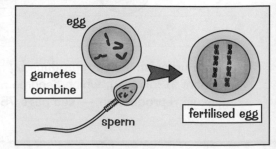

egg

gametes combine

sperm

fertilised egg

## Now that I have your undivided attention...

Remember, in humans, meiosis only occurs in <u>reproductive organs</u> where gametes are being made.

# Stem Cells and Differentiation

Stem cell research has exciting possibilities, but it's also pretty controversial.

## Embryonic Stem Cells Can Turn into ANY Type of Cell

1) Differentiation is the process by which a cell changes to become specialised for its job. In most animal cells, the ability to differentiate is lost at an early stage, but lots of plant cells don't ever lose this ability.

2) Some cells are undifferentiated. They can develop into different types of cell depending on what instructions they're given. These cells are called STEM CELLS.

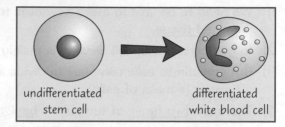

undifferentiated stem cell

differentiated white blood cell

3) Stem cells are found in early human embryos. They're exciting to doctors and medical researchers because they have the potential to turn into any kind of cell at all. This makes sense if you think about it — all the different types of cell found in a human being have to come from those few cells in the early embryo.

4) Adults also have stem cells, but they're only found in certain places, like bone marrow. These aren't as versatile as embryonic stem cells — they can't turn into any cell type at all, only certain ones.

## Stem Cells May Be Able to Cure Many Diseases

1) Medicine already uses adult stem cells to cure disease. Some blood diseases (e.g. sickle cell anaemia) can be treated by bone marrow transplants. Bone marrow contains stem cells that can turn into new blood cells to replace the faulty old ones.

2) Scientists can also extract stem cells from very early human embryos and grow them. Embryonic stem cells could be used to replace faulty cells in sick people — you could make beating heart muscle cells for people with heart disease, insulin-producing cells for people with diabetes, nerve cells for people paralysed by spinal injuries, etc.

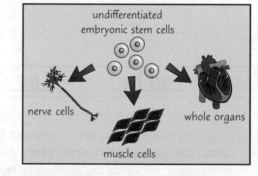

undifferentiated embryonic stem cells

nerve cells

muscle cells

whole organs

3) To get cultures of one specific type of cell, researchers try to control the differentiation of the stem cells by changing the environment they're growing in. So far, it's still a bit hit and miss — lots more research is needed.

4) Therapeutic cloning is another method of producing stem cells that is being investigated. An embryo would be produced with the same genes as the patient, so then any cells produced from this embryo would not be rejected by the patient's body if they were used for medical treatment.

## Some People Are Against Stem Cell Research

1) Some people are against stem cell research because they feel that human embryos shouldn't be used for experiments since each one is a potential human life.

2) These campaigners feel that scientists should concentrate more on finding and developing other sources of stem cells, so people could be helped without having to use embryos.

3) Others think that curing patients who already exist and who are suffering is more important than the rights of embryos. One fairly convincing argument in favour of this point of view is that the embryos used in the research are usually unwanted ones from fertility clinics which, if they weren't used for research, would probably just be destroyed.

4) In some countries stem cell research is banned, but it's allowed in the UK as long as it follows strict guidelines.

## But florists cell stems, and nobody complains about that...

The potential of stem cells is huge — but it's early days yet. Research has recently been done into getting stem cells from alternative sources. For example, some researchers think it might be possible to get cells from umbilical cords to behave like embryonic stem cells.

# Growth of Tumours

If you've ever thought you might be a hypochondriac, this page may not do you any favours.

## Cancer is Caused by Body Cells Dividing Out of Control

1) We need to be able to make new cells to grow, and so we can repair and replace damaged tissue.

2) In mature animals, cell division is mainly limited to the repair and replacement of cells.

3) But sometimes cells can start to divide in an abnormal and uncontrolled way, forming a tumour (a mass of cells).

4) There are two types of tumour — benign and malignant:

### Benign

- This is where the tumour grows until there's no more room.
- The cells stay where they are — they don't invade other tissues.
- This type of tumour isn't normally dangerous.

### Malignant

- This is where the tumour grows and can spread to healthy tissue.
- Some malignant tumour cells can get into the bloodstream and circulate to other parts of the body.
- Here, the malignant cells invade healthy tissues and form secondary tumours.
- Malignant tumours are dangerous and can be fatal.
- When we say someone has cancer, we usually mean that they have a malignant tumour.

## Tumours can be Caused by Chemicals and Radiation

1) Chemical carcinogens are chemicals that can cause cancer. For example, chemicals found in tobacco smoke and asbestos (a material that used to be used as insulation in buildings) have been linked to lung cancer. The chemicals interfere with normal cell functions, causing cells to divide uncontrollably and form a tumour.

'Carcinogen' is a big word but it just means something that causes cancer.

2) Ionising radiation such as UV (ultra violet) and X-rays can also cause cancer.

- Ionising radiation breaks molecules up into ions (charged particles).
- These ions interfere in the normal reactions going on inside the cell.
- They can cause the cell to start dividing abnormally, producing a tumour.

UV radiation from the sun is known to be the main cause of skin cancer. That's why it's important to wear sunscreen.

## Talk about ending on a depressing note...

But at least you've made it through the whole of the first section — and it was a long 'un too. Good show. There's plenty to take in here, so have a breather while you reflect on your new found knowledge. Then there's a lovely treat for you on the next page — bet you can't guess what it is...

# Revision Summary for Section One

Ta da — what a treat it is too. Some lovely questions to test how much of the section has made it into your brain. If you can't do them the first time, don't worry — just go back and brush up on the wobbly bits and have another go. Hours of fun.

1) Name five parts of a cell that both plant and animal cells have.
   What three things do plant cells have that animal cells don't?

2) Where is the genetic material found in:
   a) bacterial cells (two places),
   b) animal cells?

3) Give three ways that a palisade leaf cell is adapted for photosynthesis.

4) Give three ways that a sperm cell is adapted for swimming to an egg cell.

5) What is a tissue? What is an organ?

6) Give three examples of tissues in the human stomach, and say what job they do.

7) Name one organ system found in the human body.

8) Give two examples of plant organs and plant tissues.

9) Where are the xylem and phloem found in a root?

10) What is diffusion?

11) Name three substances that can diffuse through cell membranes, and two that can't.

12) Write a definition of the word 'osmosis'.

13) Will water molecules move into or out of a cell that is placed in:

   a) a hypotonic solution,

   b) an isotonic solution?

14) What is turgor pressure?

15) Describe an experiment that shows diffusion taking place.
    Then, as a treat, do the same for osmosis.

16) How is active transport different from diffusion in terms of:

   a) energy requirements,

   b) concentration gradients?

17) Describe how surface area to volume ratio affects the movement of substances in and out of cells.

18) Give two ways in which exchange surfaces are adapted to maximise their effectiveness.

19) Where would you find villi and what do they do?

20) In the cell nucleus, where are the genes?

21) How many pairs of chromosomes do humans have in each cell?

22) What is mitosis used for in the human body? Describe the four steps in mitosis.

23) Name the other type of cell division, and say where it happens in the body of a human male.

24) What is the name of the process in which two gametes fuse?

25) What is differentiation in a cell?

26) Give three ways that embryonic stem cells could be used to cure diseases.

27) Briefly describe what is meant by 'therapeutic cloning'.

28) Explain the difference between benign and malignant tumours.

29) Give three examples of things that can cause tumours.

# The Respiratory System

You need to get <u>oxygen</u> from the air into your bloodstream so that it can get to your cells for <u>respiration</u>. You also need to get rid of <u>carbon dioxide</u> in your blood. This all happens inside the <u>lungs</u>. Breathing is how the air gets <u>in and out</u> of your <u>lungs</u>. It's definitely a useful skill. You'll need it to get through the exam.

## The Lungs Are in the Thorax

*The <u>respiratory system</u> is a fancy way of saying the <u>breathing system</u>.*

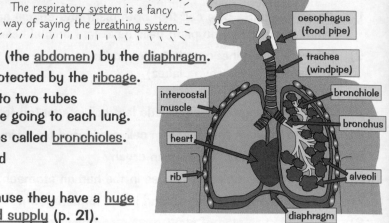

oesophagus (food pipe)
trachea (windpipe)
intercostal muscle
bronchiole
bronchus
heart
rib
alveoli
diaphragm

1) The <u>thorax</u> is the top part of your 'body'.

2) It's separated from the lower part of the body (the <u>abdomen</u>) by the <u>diaphragm</u>.

3) The lungs are like big pink <u>sponges</u> and are protected by the <u>ribcage</u>.

4) Air goes in through the <u>trachea</u>. This splits into two tubes called '<u>bronchi</u>' (each one is 'a bronchus'), one going to each lung.

5) The bronchi split into smaller and smaller tubes called <u>bronchioles</u>.

6) The bronchioles finally end at small bags called <u>alveoli</u> where the gas exchange takes place.

7) The alveoli are <u>adapted</u> for gas exchange because they have a <u>huge</u> surface area, very <u>thin</u> walls and a good <u>blood supply</u> (p. 21).

## Ventilation is Breathing In...

1) The <u>intercostal muscles</u> contract, pulling the ribcage up.

2) The <u>diaphragm contracts</u> and flattens out.

3) Thorax volume <u>increases</u>.

4) This <u>decreases</u> the air pressure <u>inside</u> the lungs, so it's <u>less</u> than the air pressure <u>outside</u>. This draws air <u>in</u>.

## ...and Breathing Out

1) The <u>intercostal muscles</u> relax, so the ribcage moves down.

2) The <u>diaphragm relaxes</u> and becomes dome-shaped again.

3) Thorax volume <u>decreases</u>.

4) This <u>increases</u> the pressure, so air <u>leaves</u> the lungs.

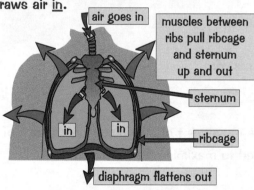

air goes in
muscles between ribs pull ribcage and sternum up and out
sternum
ribcage
in    in
diaphragm flattens out

*Inhale means breathe in. Exhale means breathe out.*

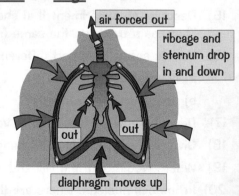

air forced out
ribcage and sternum drop in and down
out    out
diaphragm moves up

## Artificial Ventilators Help People to Breathe

1) Healthy people breathe <u>automatically</u>, <u>24 hours a day</u>. However, some people <u>can't breathe</u> by themselves, e.g. if they're under <u>general anaesthetic</u>, or have a <u>lung injury</u> or <u>disease</u>. These people need <u>ventilators</u> — machines that move air (often with extra oxygen added in) <u>into</u> or <u>out of</u> the <u>lungs</u>.

2) There are <u>two types</u> of ventilator — negative pressure ventilators and positive pressure ventilators.

3) A <u>negative pressure</u> ventilator uses a <u>sealed case</u> placed around a patient's chest. Air is <u>pumped out</u> of the case, so the <u>pressure drops</u> around the chest. This makes the lungs <u>expand</u> and air is <u>drawn into</u> them. Air is then pumped <u>into</u> the case to produce the opposite effect — air <u>leaves</u> the lungs.

4) A <u>positive pressure</u> ventilator works by <u>pumping air into</u> the lungs, which <u>expands</u> the ribcage. When it stops pumping, the ribcage <u>relaxes</u> and pushes air back <u>out</u> of the lungs.

## Stop huffing and puffing and just LEARN IT...

When you breathe in, you don't suck the air in. You make the space in your lungs <u>bigger</u> and the air rushes in to fill it. The <u>alveoli</u> are where the <u>oxygen</u> gets into the blood supply and the waste <u>carbon dioxide</u> gets out.

# Respiration

You need <u>energy</u> to keep your body going. Energy comes from <u>food</u>, and it's <u>released</u> by <u>respiration</u>.

## Respiration is NOT "Breathing In and Out"

<u>Respiration</u> involves many reactions. These are really important reactions, as respiration releases the <u>energy</u> that the cell needs to do just about everything.

1) <u>Respiration</u> is <u>not</u> breathing in and breathing out, as you might think.

2) <u>Respiration</u> is the process of <u>releasing energy</u> from the <u>breakdown of glucose</u> (sugar) — and it goes on in <u>every cell</u> in your body.

3) It happens in <u>plants</u> too. <u>All</u> living things <u>respire</u>. It's how they release <u>energy</u> from their <u>food</u>.

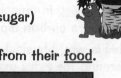

> **RESPIRATION** is the process of <u>RELEASING ENERGY FROM GLUCOSE</u>, which goes on <u>IN EVERY CELL</u>

## Aerobic Respiration Needs Plenty of Oxygen

1) <u>Aerobic respiration</u> is respiration using <u>oxygen</u>. It's the most <u>efficient</u> way to release energy from glucose. (You can also have <u>anaerobic</u> respiration, which happens <u>without</u> oxygen, but that doesn't release nearly as much energy — see page 30.)

2) Aerobic respiration goes on <u>all the time</u> in <u>plants</u> and <u>animals</u>.

3) Most of the reactions in <u>aerobic respiration</u> happen inside <u>mitochondria</u> (see page 12).

4) You need to learn the <u>word</u> and <u>symbol equations</u> for aerobic respiration:

> **Glucose + oxygen ➡ carbon dioxide + water ( + ENERGY )**
>
> $$C_6H_{12}O_6 + 6O_2 \longrightarrow 6CO_2 + 6H_2O \ (+ ENERGY)$$

## Respiration Releases Energy for All Kinds of Things

You need to learn these <u>four examples</u> of what the <u>energy</u> released by aerobic respiration is used for:

1) To build up <u>larger molecules</u> from <u>smaller</u> ones (like proteins from amino acids).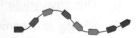

2) In animals it's used to allow the <u>muscles</u> to <u>contract</u> (so they can <u>move</u> about).

3) In <u>mammals</u> and <u>birds</u> the energy is used to keep their <u>body temperature</u> steady in colder surroundings. (Unlike other animals, mammals and birds keep their bodies constantly warm.)

4) In <u>plants</u> it's used to build <u>sugars</u>, <u>nitrates</u> and other nutrients into <u>amino acids</u>, which are then built up into <u>proteins</u>.

## <u>Don't stop respirin' — hold on to that feelin'...</u>

Isn't it strange to think that <u>each individual living cell</u> in your body is <u>respiring</u> every <u>second</u> of every day, releasing energy from the food you eat. Next time someone accuses you of being lazy you could claim that you're busy respiring — it's enough to make anyone feel tired. As tired as cheesy 80s pop songs.

# Respiration and Exercise

When you exercise, your body quickly adapts so that your muscles get <u>more oxygen and glucose</u> to supply <u>energy</u>. If your body can't get enough oxygen or glucose to them, it has some back-up plans ready.

## Exercise Increases the Heart Rate

1) Muscles are made of <u>muscle cells</u>. These use <u>oxygen</u> to <u>release energy</u> from <u>glucose</u> (<u>aerobic respiration</u> — see page 29), which is used to <u>contract</u> the muscles.

2) An <u>increase</u> in muscle activity requires <u>more glucose and oxygen</u> to be supplied to the muscle cells, and extra carbon dioxide ($CO_2$) to be <u>removed</u>. For this to happen the blood has to flow at a <u>faster</u> rate.

3) This is why physical activity <u>increases</u> your <u>breathing rate</u> and makes you breathe <u>more deeply</u> to meet the demand for <u>extra oxygen</u>, and it <u>increases</u> the speed at which the <u>heart pumps</u> to increase blood flow.

4) An <u>unfit</u> person has a <u>higher resting heart rate</u> than a fit person — at rest, their heart beats faster.

5) An unfit person's heart rate also <u>goes up</u> a lot <u>more</u> during <u>exercise</u> and they take longer to <u>recover</u> (for their heart rate to return to the resting rate afterwards).

## Glycogen is Used During Exercise

1) Some <u>glucose</u> from food is <u>stored</u> as <u>glycogen</u>.

2) Glycogen's mainly stored in the liver, but each <u>muscle</u> also has its own store.

3) During vigorous exercise muscles use glucose <u>rapidly</u>, so some of the stored glycogen is converted back to <u>glucose</u> to provide more energy.

## Anaerobic Respiration is Used if There's Not Enough Oxygen

1) When you do vigorous exercise and your body can't supply enough <u>oxygen</u> to your muscles, they start doing <u>anaerobic respiration</u> instead of aerobic respiration.

2) "Anaerobic" just means "<u>without</u> oxygen". It's the <u>incomplete</u> breakdown of glucose, which produces <u>lactic acid</u>.

$$glucose \rightarrow lactic\ acid\ (+\ energy)$$
$$C_6H_{12}O_6 \rightarrow 2C_3H_6O_3\ (+\ energy)$$

3) This is <u>**NOT the best way** to convert glucose into energy</u> because <u>lactic acid</u> builds up in the muscles, which gets <u>painful</u>. It also causes <u>muscle fatigue</u> — the muscles get <u>tired</u> and then <u>stop contracting efficiently</u>.

4) Another downside is that <u>anaerobic respiration</u> does <u>not release nearly as much energy</u> as aerobic respiration — but it's useful in emergencies.

5) The <u>advantage</u> is that at least you can keep on using your muscles for a while longer.

6) <u>Plants</u> and some <u>microorganisms</u> can respire <u>without oxygen</u> too, but they produce <u>ethanol</u> (alcohol) and $CO_2$ <u>instead</u> of lactic acid.

## Anaerobic Respiration Leads to an Oxygen Debt

1) After resorting to anaerobic respiration, when you stop exercising you'll have an "<u>oxygen debt</u>".

2) In other words you have to "<u>repay</u>" the oxygen that you didn't get to your muscles in time, because your <u>lungs</u>, <u>heart</u> and <u>blood</u> couldn't keep up with the <u>demand</u> earlier on.

3) This means you have to keep breathing hard for a while <u>after you stop</u>, to get <u>more oxygen</u> into your blood. Blood flows through your muscles to <u>remove</u> the lactic acid by <u>oxidising</u> it to harmless $CO_2$ and water.

4) While <u>high levels</u> of $CO_2$ and <u>lactic acid</u> are detected in the blood (by the brain), the <u>pulse</u> and <u>breathing rate</u> stay high to try and rectify the situation.

## Oxygen debt — cheap to pay back...

Phew... bet you're exhausted after reading this. Still, it needs learning before you have a pit stop. In the exam, you could be asked to <u>interpret data</u> on the <u>effects of exercise</u> on the body — so make sure you <u>know this page</u>.

# Circulatory System — The Heart

The circulatory system's main function is to get <u>food and oxygen</u> to every cell in the body. As well as being a delivery service, it's also a waste collection service — it carries <u>waste products</u> like <u>carbon dioxide</u> and <u>urea</u> to where they can be removed from the body.

## The DOUBLE Circulatory System, Actually

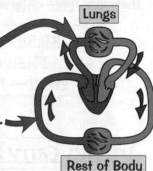

The circulatory system is made up of the <u>heart</u>, <u>blood vessels</u> and <u>blood</u>. Humans have a <u>double circulatory system</u> — <u>two circuits</u> joined together:

1) The first one pumps <u>deoxygenated</u> blood (blood without oxygen) to the <u>lungs</u> to take in <u>oxygen</u>. The blood then <u>returns</u> to the heart.

2) The second one pumps <u>oxygenated</u> blood around <u>all the other organs</u> of the <u>body</u>. The blood <u>gives up</u> its oxygen at the body cells and the <u>deoxygenated</u> blood <u>returns</u> to the heart to be pumped out to the <u>lungs</u> again.

## The Heart Contracts to Pump Blood Around The Body

1) The <u>heart</u> is a pumping <u>organ</u> that keeps the blood flowing around the body. The walls of the heart are mostly made of <u>muscle tissue</u>.

2) The heart has <u>valves</u> to make sure that blood flows in the right direction — they prevent it flowing <u>backwards</u>.

3) This is how the <u>heart</u> uses its <u>four chambers</u> (right atrium, right ventricle, left atrium and left ventricle) to pump blood around:

1) <u>Blood flows into</u> the two <u>atria</u> from the <u>vena cava</u> and the <u>pulmonary vein</u>.
2) The <u>atria contract</u>, pushing the blood into the <u>ventricles</u>.
3) The <u>ventricles contract</u>, forcing the blood into the <u>pulmonary artery</u> and the <u>aorta</u>, and <u>out</u> of the <u>heart</u>.
4) The blood then flows to the <u>organs</u> through <u>arteries</u>, and <u>returns</u> through <u>veins</u> (see next page).
5) The atria fill again and the whole cycle <u>starts over</u>.

Atrium is when there is just one. Atria is plural.

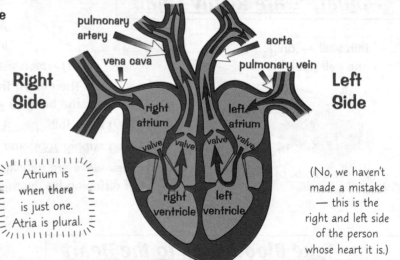

(No, we haven't made a mistake — this is the right and left side of the person whose heart it is.)

## The Heart Has a Pacemaker

1) Your resting heart rate is <u>controlled</u> by a group of cells in the right atrium wall that act as a <u>pacemaker</u>.

2) These cells produce a small <u>electric impulse</u> which spreads to the surrounding muscle cells, causing them to <u>contract</u>.

3) An <u>artificial pacemaker</u> is often used to control heartbeat if the natural pacemaker cells don't work properly (e.g. if the patient has an <u>irregular heartbeat</u>). It's a little device that's implanted under the skin and has a wire going to the heart. It produces an <u>electric current</u> to keep the heart <u>beating regularly</u>.

## Okay — let's get to the heart of the matter...

The human heart beats <u>100 000 times a day</u> on average. You can feel a <u>pulse</u> in your wrist or neck (this is where the vessels are close to the surface). Your pulse is the <u>blood</u> being pushed along by another beat. Doctors use a <u>stethoscope</u> to listen to your heart — it's actually the <u>valves closing</u> that they hear though.

# Circulatory System — Blood Vessels

Want to know <u>more</u> about the <u>circulatory system</u>... Good. Because here's a whole extra page.

## Blood Vessels are Designed for Their Function

There are <u>three</u> different types of <u>blood vessel</u>:

> 1) <u>ARTERIES</u> — these carry the blood <u>away</u> from the heart to the <u>organs</u> and <u>tissues</u>.
> 2) <u>CAPILLARIES</u> — these are involved in the <u>exchange of materials</u> in the organs and tissues.
> 3) <u>VEINS</u> — these carry the blood <u>back to</u> the heart.

## Arteries Carry Blood Under Pressure

1) The heart pumps the blood out at <u>high pressure</u> so the artery walls are <u>strong</u> and <u>elastic</u>.

2) The walls are <u>thick</u> compared to the size of the hole down the middle (the "<u>lumen</u>" — silly name!).

3) They contain thick layers of <u>muscle</u> to make them <u>strong</u>, and <u>elastic fibres</u> to allow them to stretch and <u>spring back</u>.

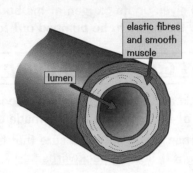

elastic fibres and smooth muscle

lumen

## Capillaries are Really Small

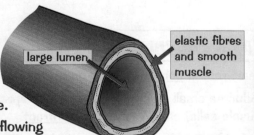

thin wall — only one cell thick

very small lumen

nucleus of cell

1) Arteries branch into <u>capillaries</u> in the organs and tissues.

2) Capillaries are really <u>narrow</u>, and so are too small to see.

3) They carry the blood <u>really close</u> to <u>every cell</u> in the body to <u>exchange substances</u> with them.

4) They have thin, <u>permeable</u> walls, so substances can <u>diffuse</u> in and out.

5) They supply <u>food</u> and <u>oxygen</u>, and take away <u>waste</u> like <u>$CO_2$</u>.

6) Their walls are usually <u>only one cell thick</u>. This <u>increases</u> the rate of diffusion by <u>decreasing</u> the <u>distance</u> over which it occurs.

## Veins Take Blood Back to the Heart

1) Capillaries eventually <u>join up</u> to form <u>veins</u>.

2) The blood is at <u>lower pressure</u> in the veins so the walls don't need to be as <u>thick</u> as artery walls.

3) They have a <u>bigger lumen</u> than arteries to help the blood <u>flow</u> despite the lower pressure.

4) They also have <u>valves</u> to help keep the blood flowing in the <u>right direction</u> — they prevent back-flow.

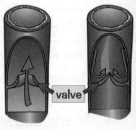

large lumen

elastic fibres and smooth muscle

valve

## Learn this page — don't struggle in vein...

Here's an interesting fact for you — your body contains about <u>60 000 miles</u> of blood vessels. That's about <u>six times</u> the distance from <u>London</u> to <u>Sydney</u> in Australia. Of course, capillaries are really tiny, which is how there can be such a big length — they can only be seen with a <u>microscope</u>, not just using your eyes.

# Circulatory System — The Blood

Blood is a <u>tissue</u>. One of its jobs is to act as a huge <u>transport system</u>. There are four main things in blood...

## Red Blood Cells Carry Oxygen

1) The job of red blood cells is to carry <u>oxygen</u> from the lungs to all the cells in the body.

2) They have a doughnut shape to give a <u>large surface area</u> for absorbing <u>oxygen</u>.

3) They <u>don't</u> have a nucleus — this allows more room to carry oxygen.

4) They contain a red pigment called <u>haemoglobin</u>.

5) In the <u>lungs</u>, oxygen diffuses from the alveoli into the blood. Haemoglobin in the red blood cells combines with <u>oxygen</u> to become <u>oxyhaemoglobin</u>.

6) Then, in <u>body tissues</u>, the reverse happens — oxyhaemoglobin splits up into haemoglobin and oxygen, <u>releasing the oxygen</u> which <u>diffuses</u> into the <u>cells</u>.

> The more red blood cells you've got, the more oxygen that can get to your cells. At high altitudes there's less oxygen in the air — so people who live there produce more red blood cells to compensate.

## White Blood Cells Defend Against Disease

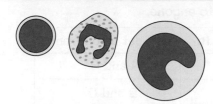

1) They can change shape to gobble up unwelcome <u>microorganisms</u>.

2) They produce <u>antibodies</u> to fight microorganisms, as well as <u>antitoxins</u> to neutralise any toxins produced by the microorganisms.

3) Unlike red blood cells, they <u>do</u> have a <u>nucleus</u>.

## Platelets Help Blood Clot

1) These are <u>small fragments</u> of <u>cells</u>. They have <u>no nucleus</u>.

2) They help the blood to <u>clot</u> at a wound — to stop all your <u>blood pouring out</u> and to stop <u>microorganisms</u> getting in.

3) Blood clotting involves many reactions, all of which are <u>controlled</u> by <u>enzymes</u>. During these reactions <u>fibrinogen</u> (a <u>soluble protein</u>) is changed into <u>fibrin</u> (solid <u>insoluble fibres</u>). The fibrin fibres <u>tangle together</u> and form a <u>mesh</u> in which <u>platelets</u> and <u>red blood cells</u> get trapped — this forms the clot. (So basically platelets just float about waiting for accidents to happen.)

4) A <u>lack</u> of platelets can cause excessive bleeding and bruising.

## Plasma is the Liquid That Carries Everything in Blood

This is a pale straw-coloured liquid which <u>carries just about everything</u>:

1) <u>Red</u> and <u>white blood cells</u> and <u>platelets</u>.

2) Nutrients like <u>glucose</u> and <u>amino acids</u>. These are the <u>soluble products</u> of <u>digestion</u> which are absorbed from the gut and taken to the cells of the body.

3) <u>Carbon dioxide</u> from the organs to the lungs.

4) <u>Urea</u> from the liver to the kidneys.

5) <u>Hormones</u>.

6) <u>Antibodies</u> and <u>antitoxins</u> produced by the white blood cells.

## Platelets — ideal for small dinners...

When you're <u>ill</u> the doctor often takes a <u>blood sample</u> for analysis. Blood tests can be used to diagnose loads of things — <u>not</u> just disorders of the blood. This is because the blood transports <u>so many chemicals</u> produced by <u>so many organs</u>... and it's easier to take blood than, say, a piece of muscle (even if it's not much fun).

# Blood Type and Organ Donation

If you get badly hurt or have a serious illness, you might need a blood transfusion or an organ donation.

## Blood Type is Important in Transfusions

1) If you're in an accident or having surgery, you may lose a lot of blood — this needs to be replaced by a blood transfusion, using blood from a blood donor. But you can't just use any old blood...

2) People have different blood groups or types — you can be any one of: A, B, O or AB. These letters refer to the type of antigens on the surface of a person's red blood cells. Antigens are proteins on the surface of cells. They can trigger a response from a person's immune system.

3) Red blood cells can have A or B antigens (or neither, or both) on their surface.

4) And blood plasma can contain anti-A or anti-B antibodies. (See previous page for more on plasma.)

5) If an anti-A antibody meets an A antigen, the blood clumps together. This is known as agglutination (and it's not good). The same thing happens when an anti-B antibody meets a B antigen. The antibodies are acting as agglutinins — or 'things that make stuff clump together'.

6) Agglutination is bad, so we don't want it to happen. This means that your blood type decides what type of blood you can receive in a transfusion.

*There's more on antibodies on page 53.*

7) This table explains which blood groups can donate blood to which other blood groups. It shows that blood group O is the universal donor — it can be given to anyone.

| Blood Group | Antigens | Antibodies | Can give blood to | Can get blood from |
|---|---|---|---|---|
| A | A | anti-B | A and AB | A and O |
| B | B | anti-A | B and AB | B and O |
| AB | A, B | none | only AB | anyone |
| O | none | anti-A, anti-B | anyone | only O |

For example, if your blood group is type O, your blood can be given to anyone — there are no antigens on your blood cells, so any anti-A or anti-B antibodies have nothing to 'attack'. You can only receive blood from other type O people though — your antibodies would attack the antigens in type A, B or AB blood.

## Transplanted Organs can be Rejected by the Body

1) If an organ is severely damaged, it can sometimes be removed and replaced by one from someone else — this known as an organ transplant.

2) Healthy organs are usually transplanted from people who have died suddenly, say in a car accident, and who are on the organ donor register or carry a donor card (provided their relatives give the go-ahead).

3) However, the donor organ can be rejected by the patient's immune system — the foreign antigens (i.e. ones not recognised by their own immune system) on the donor organ are attacked by the patient's antibodies.

4) To help prevent rejection, precautions are taken:
   - A donor with a tissue-type that closely matches the patient is chosen. Tissue-type is based on antigens, so people with similar tissue-types will have similar antigens.
   - The patient is treated with drugs that suppress the immune system, so that their immune system won't attack the transplanted organ.

## I think I need an information transfusion...

You might get asked a question on who can donate blood to whom in the exam. Just look at what blood type the donor is and think about what antigens and antibodies they have in their blood. You could also be given some information about treating organ failure with mechanical devices (see p. 35) or transplants and asked about the pros and cons of each. Just make sure you know this stuff really well to help you out if it comes up.

# Circulation Aids

This page is about <u>artificial hearts</u> and <u>heart valves</u>, and <u>stents</u> (tiny tube-ey things that keep arteries open). All a bit gruesome, I'll admit — but it's life-saving stuff.

## An Artificial Heart Can Pump Blood Around the Body

1) <u>Artificial hearts</u> are <u>mechanical</u> devices that are put into a person to <u>pump blood</u> if their own heart <u>fails</u>. They're usually used as a <u>temporary</u> fix, to keep a person <u>alive</u> until a <u>donor heart</u> can be found or to help a person <u>recover</u> by allowing the heart to <u>rest</u> and <u>heal</u>. In some cases though they're used as a <u>permanent</u> fix, which <u>reduces</u> the <u>need</u> for a donor heart.

2) The main <u>advantage</u> of artificial hearts is that they're <u>less likely to be rejected</u> by the body's immune system. This is because they're made from <u>metals</u> or <u>plastics</u>, so the body doesn't recognise them as '<u>foreign</u>' and attack in the same way as it does with living tissue.

3) But <u>surgery</u> to fit an artificial heart can lead to <u>bleeding</u> and <u>infection</u>. Also, artificial hearts <u>don't</u> work as well as healthy <u>natural</u> ones — parts of the heart could <u>wear out</u> or the <u>electrical motor</u> could <u>fail</u>. Blood doesn't flow through artificial hearts as <u>smoothly</u>, which can cause <u>blood clots</u> and lead to <u>strokes</u>. The patient has to take <u>drugs</u> to <u>thin</u> their blood and make sure this doesn't happen, which can cause problems with <u>bleeding</u> if they're <u>hurt</u> in an accident.

## Artificial Valves can be Biological or Mechanical

1) The <u>valves</u> in the heart can be damaged or weakened by <u>heart attacks</u>, <u>infection</u> or <u>old age</u>.

2) The damage may cause the <u>valve tissue</u> to <u>stiffen</u>, so it <u>won't open properly</u>. Or a valve may become <u>leaky</u>, allowing blood to flow in <u>both directions</u> rather than just forward. This means that blood <u>doesn't circulate</u> as <u>effectively</u> as normal.

3) Severe valve damage can be treated by <u>replacing</u> the valve with an <u>artificial one</u>. Artificial valves can be ones taken from <u>humans</u> or <u>other mammals</u> (e.g. cows, pigs) — these are <u>biological valves</u>. Or they can be <u>man-made</u> — these are <u>mechanical valves</u>.

4) Replacing a <u>valve</u> is a much <u>less drastic</u> procedure than a whole heart transplant. But fitting artificial valves is still <u>major surgery</u> and there can still be problems with <u>blood clots</u>.

## Stents Keep Arteries Open

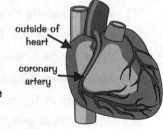

outside of heart

coronary artery

1) <u>Coronary heart disease</u> is when the <u>coronary arteries</u> that supply the <u>blood</u> to the muscle of the heart get <u>blocked</u> by <u>fatty deposits</u>. This causes the arteries to become <u>narrow</u>, so blood flow is <u>restricted</u> and there's a <u>lack of oxygen</u> to the heart muscle — this can result in a <u>heart attack</u>.

2) <u>Stents</u> are <u>tubes</u> that are inserted <u>inside arteries</u>. They keep them <u>open</u>, making sure <u>blood can pass through</u> to the heart muscles. This keeps the person's <u>heart beating</u> (and the person alive).

deposits of fat build up

normal artery

space in centre of artery shrinks, so it's harder for blood to pass through

stent pushes artery wall out, squashing fatty deposit

more space in the centre of the artery

3) <u>Stents</u> are a way of <u>lowering</u> the <u>risk</u> of a <u>heart attack</u> in people with <u>coronary heart disease</u>.

4) But <u>over time</u>, the artery can <u>narrow</u> again as stents can <u>irritate</u> the artery and make <u>scar tissue</u> grow. The patient also has to take <u>drugs</u> to stop <u>blood clotting</u> on the stent.

## Pity they can't fit me an artificial brain before the exam...

In your exam they may ask you to consider the <u>advantages</u> and <u>disadvantages</u> of these treatments. Obviously, if you're <u>really ill</u>, you're not going to <u>turn down</u> a stent or an artificial valve — but these treatments <u>aren't perfect</u>.

# Revision Summary for Section Two

So you think you've learnt all these important processes and treatments, eh... Well, there's only one way to really find out. And you know what that is, I'll bet. It's obvious... I mean, there's a whole load of questions staring you in the face — chances are, it's got to involve those in some way. And sure enough, it does. Just write down the answers to all these questions. Then go back over the section and see if you got any wrong. If you did, then you need a bit more revision, so go back and have another read of the section and then have another go. It's the best way to make sure you actually know your stuff.

1) Explain how alveoli are adapted for efficient gas exchange.
2) Describe what happens during ventilation.
3) Explain how negative pressure ventilators work.
4) Name one other type of modern ventilator. Explain how they work.
5) Where in the cell do most of the reactions in aerobic respiration happen?
6) Write down the word equation for aerobic respiration.
7) Write down the symbol equation for aerobic respiration.
8) Give two examples of how an animal uses the energy released by aerobic respiration.
9) What happens to our breathing and heart rate during exercise? Why?
10) What is anaerobic respiration? Give the word equation for anaerobic respiration in our bodies.
11) Some plants and microorganisms respire anaerobically. Name the two substances this process produces.
12) Explain how you repay an oxygen debt.
13) Name the three parts of our circulation system.
14) What are the walls of the heart mostly made of?
15) Give the function of the following parts of the heart:    a) atria    b) ventricles    c) valves
16) What is an artificial pacemaker? What does it do?
17) Why do arteries need very muscular, elastic walls?
18) Explain how capillaries are adapted to their function.
19) Where do veins carry blood to and from?
20) What's the red substance in red blood cells called? What is it called when it combines with oxygen?
21) What do white blood cells do?
22) What are the cell fragments called that help blood to clot?
23) What happens when blood clots?
24) Name three things blood plasma transports.
25) What are antigens?
26) Which blood group is the universal donor?
27) Explain what would happen if a person with type A blood was given a transfusion of type B blood.
28) Give two precautions that are taken to prevent a patient from rejecting a transplanted organ.
29) What are artificial hearts?
30) Give two reasons why a person may need an artificial heart valve.
31) Name the two types of artificial heart valve.
32) What is coronary heart disease?
33) What does a stent do?

# Carbohydrates, Lipids and Proteins

You __eat__ and __digest__ (break down) biological molecules like __carbohydrates__, __lipids__ and __proteins__. They're generally __long__, __complex molecules__ made up from __smaller basic units__, as you'll find out below...

## You Need to Know the Structure of Carbohydrates, Lipids and Proteins

### Carbohydrates are Made Up of Sugar Units

- __Carbohydrate__ molecules are made up of __units of sugar__.
- __Simple sugars__ are carbohydrates that are only made up of __one__ or __two__ units of sugar, e.g. __glucose__ is made up of __one unit__ of sugar, __sucrose__ is made up of __two units__ of sugar.
- __Large__, __complex carbohydrates__ such as __starch__ and __cellulose__ are made up of many __smaller sugar units__ (e.g. __glucose__ or __sucrose__ molecules) joined together in a __long chain__.

Glucose → Starch

and other simple sugars, e.g. sucrose

### Lipids are Made Up of Fatty Acids and Glycerol

- __Lipids__ (fats and oils) are built from __fatty acids__ and __glycerol__.
- A lipid molecule contains __one__ molecule of __glycerol__ joined to __three fatty acid molecules__.

Glycerol & fatty acids → Lipid

### Proteins are Made Up of Amino Acids

- __Proteins__ are made up of __long chains__ of __amino acids__.
- These chains are __folded__ into __specific shapes__ that allow other molecules to fit into the protein.

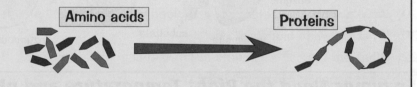

Amino acids → Proteins

## Proteins Have Many Different Functions

There are __hundreds__ of __different proteins__ and they all have __different functions__. Here are __four examples__ that you need to know about:

1) ANTIBODIES — help the body to __fight disease__. These proteins are part of your __immune system__ and are produced by __white blood cells__ (see page 33).

2) HORMONES — are used to __carry messages__ around the body. E.g. __insulin__ is a hormone released into the blood by the pancreas to __regulate__ the __blood sugar level__ (see page 51).

3) STRUCTURAL PROTEINS — make up tissues in the body such as __muscles__.

4) ENZYMES — __control__ chemical __reactions__ in the body. Enzymes have __unique__ __shapes__ so that only __certain__ molecules can __fit__ into them (see next page).

## Biological molecules — a bit like LEGO® really...

Make sure you know what __carbohydrates__, __lipids__ and __proteins__ are made up of — it'll make the stuff coming up on enzymes and digestion a lot easier. Right, onwards and upwards... Or maybe just over the page...

# Enzymes

Chemical reactions are what make you work. And enzymes are what make them work.

## Enzymes Are Catalysts Produced by Living Things

1) Living things have thousands of different chemical reactions going on inside them all the time. These reactions need to be carefully controlled — to get the right amounts of substances.

2) You can usually make a reaction happen more quickly by raising the temperature. This would speed up the useful reactions but also the unwanted ones too... not good. There's also a limit to how far you can raise the temperature inside a living creature before its cells start getting damaged.

3) So... living things produce enzymes that act as biological catalysts. Enzymes reduce the need for high temperatures and we only have enzymes to speed up the useful chemical reactions in the body.

> A **CATALYST** is a substance which **INCREASES** the speed of a reaction, without being **CHANGED** or **USED UP** in the reaction.

4) Enzymes are all protein chains that are folded into the unique shapes that the enzymes need to do their jobs (see below).

## Enzymes Have Special Shapes So They Can Catalyse Reactions

1) Chemical reactions usually involve things either being split apart or joined together.

2) A substrate is a molecule that is changed in a reaction.

3) Every enzyme molecule has an active site — the part where a substrate joins on to the enzyme.

4) Enzymes are really picky — they usually only catalyse one reaction.

5) This is because, for the enzyme to work, the substrate has to be the correct shape to fit its active site — if it doesn't, the reaction won't be catalysed.

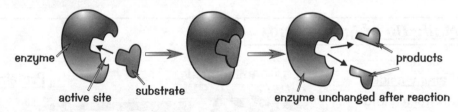

enzyme    active site    substrate    products    enzyme unchanged after reaction

## Enzymes Need the Right Temperature and pH

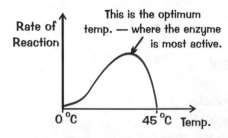

Rate of Reaction

This is the optimum temp. — where the enzyme is most active.

0 °C    45 °C  Temp.

1) Changing the temperature changes the rate of an enzyme-catalysed reaction.

2) A higher temperature increases the rate at first. But if it gets too hot, some of the bonds holding the enzyme together break. This changes the enzyme's active site so the substrate won't fit any more and the enzyme won't work. It's said to be denatured.

3) Enzymes in the human body normally work best at around 37 °C.

4) The pH also affects enzymes. If it's too high or too low, the pH interferes with the bonds holding the enzyme together. This changes the active site and denatures the enzyme.

5) All enzymes have a different optimum pH (pH they work best at). It's often neutral pH 7, but not always — e.g. pepsin is an enzyme that breaks down proteins in the stomach. It works best at pH 2, so it's well-suited to the acidic conditions there.

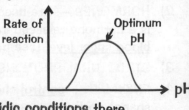

Rate of reaction    Optimum pH    pH

## If only enzymes could speed up revision...

Just like you've got to have the correct key for a lock, you've got to have the right substance for an enzyme. If the substance doesn't fit, the enzyme won't catalyse the reaction...

# Enzymes and Digestion

Not all enzymes work inside body cells — some work <u>outside</u> cells.  For example, the enzymes used in <u>digestion</u> are produced by cells and then <u>released</u> into the <u>gut</u> to <u>mix</u> with <u>food</u>.  Makes sense, really.

## Digestive Enzymes Break Down Big Molecules into Smaller Ones

1)  <u>Starch</u>, <u>proteins</u> and <u>lipids</u> are BIG, <u>insoluble</u> molecules.
    They're too big to pass through the walls of the digestive system.

2)  <u>Sugars</u>, <u>amino acids</u>, <u>glycerol</u> and <u>fatty acids</u> are much smaller, <u>soluble</u> molecules.
    They can pass easily through the walls of the digestive system.

3)  The <u>digestive enzymes</u> break down the BIG, insoluble molecules into the smaller, soluble ones.
    These can then be <u>absorbed</u> into the <u>bloodstream</u> through the <u>wall</u> of the <u>small intestine</u>.

### Amylase Converts Starch into Sugars

Amylase works in the <u>mouth</u> and <u>small intestine</u>. It breaks <u>starch</u> down into <u>sugars</u>.

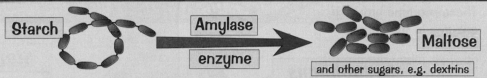

Amylase is made in <u>three</u> places:
1)  The <u>salivary glands</u>
2)  The <u>pancreas</u>
3)  The <u>small intestine</u>

### Protease Converts Proteins into Amino Acids

Protease works in the <u>stomach</u> and <u>small intestine</u>. It breaks <u>proteins</u> down into <u>amino acids</u>.

Protease is made in <u>three</u> places:
1)  The <u>stomach</u> (it's called <u>pepsin</u> there)
2)  The <u>pancreas</u>
3)  The <u>small intestine</u>

### Lipase Converts Lipids into Glycerol and Fatty Acids

Lipase works in the <u>small intestine</u>. It breaks <u>lipids</u> down into <u>fatty acids</u> and <u>glycerol</u>.

 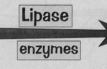 

Lipase is made in <u>two</u> places:
1)  The <u>pancreas</u>
2)  The <u>small intestine</u>

*Remember, lipids are fats and oils.*

## Bile Neutralises the Stomach Acid and Emulsifies Fats

1)  Bile is <u>produced</u> in the <u>liver</u>.  It's <u>stored</u> in the <u>gall bladder</u> before it's released into the <u>small intestine</u>.

2)  The <u>hydrochloric acid</u> in the stomach makes the pH <u>too acidic</u> for enzymes in the small intestine to work properly.  Bile is <u>alkaline</u> — it <u>neutralises</u> the acid and makes conditions <u>alkaline</u>. The enzymes in the small intestine <u>work best</u> in these alkaline conditions.

3)  Bile also <u>emulsifies</u> fats.  In other words it breaks the fat into <u>tiny droplets</u>.  This gives a much <u>bigger surface area</u> of fat for the enzyme lipase to work on — which makes its digestion <u>faster</u>.

## What do you call an acid that's eaten all the pies...

This all happens inside our digestive system, but there are some microorganisms that secrete their digestive enzymes <u>outside their body</u> onto the food.  The food's digested, then the microorganism absorbs the nutrients. Nice.  I wouldn't like to empty the contents of my stomach onto my plate before eating it.

# More on Enzymes and Digestion

So now you know what the enzymes do, here's a nice big picture of the whole of the digestive system.

## The Breakdown of Food is Catalysed by Enzymes

1) Enzymes used in the digestive system are produced by specialised cells in glands and in the gut lining.

2) The enzymes move out of these cells and into the digestive system where they get to work on the food.

3) As you've seen on the previous page, different enzymes catalyse the breakdown of different food molecules in different parts of the digestive system.

4) You need to know where the different organs of the digestive system are and what they do.

Tongue

### Salivary glands

These produce amylase enzyme in the saliva.

### Oesophagus

The muscular tube that connects the mouth and the stomach.

### Liver

Where bile is produced. Bile neutralises stomach acid and emulsifies fats.

### Gall bladder

Where bile is stored, before it's released into the small intestine.

### Duodenum

The first section of the small intestine. Enzymes from the pancreas end up here.

### Small intestine

1) Produces protease, amylase and lipase enzymes to complete digestion.

2) This is also where the digested food is absorbed out of the digestive system into the blood.

### Stomach

1) It pummels the food with its muscular walls.

2) It produces the protease enzyme, pepsin.

3) It produces hydrochloric acid for two reasons:
   • To kill bacteria
   • To give the right pH for the protease enzyme to work (pH 2 — acidic).

### Pancreas

Produces protease, amylase and lipase enzymes. It releases these into the duodenum.

### Large intestine

Where a lot of the water that's mixed in with the food is absorbed into the bloodstream.

### Anus

Where faeces (mainly made up of indigestible food) bid you a fond farewell.

## Mmmm — so who's for a chocolate digestive...

Did you know that the whole of your digestive system is actually a hole that goes right through your body. Think about it. It just gets loads of food, digestive juices and enzymes piled into it. Most of it's then absorbed into the body and the rest is politely stored ready for removal.

*Section Three — Enzymes and Digestion*

# Uses of Enzymes

Some <u>microorganisms</u> produce enzymes which pass <u>out</u> of their cells and catalyse reactions outside them (e.g. to <u>digest</u> the microorganism's <u>food</u>). These enzymes have many <u>uses</u> in the <u>home</u> and in <u>industry</u>.

## Enzymes Are Used in Biological Detergents in the Home

1) Some stains are caused by <u>soluble</u> chemicals and so they <u>wash out</u> easily in water. Stubborn stains contain <u>insoluble chemicals</u> like proteins and fats. They don't wash out with just water.

2) <u>Non-biological detergents</u> contain <u>chemicals</u> that break up <u>stains</u> on your clothes.

3) <u>Biological detergents</u> contain the same chemicals as non-biological ones, but also contain a mixture of <u>enzymes</u> which break down the stubborn stains.

4) Because the enzymes break down <u>animal</u> and <u>plant</u> matter, they're ideal for removing <u>stains</u> like <u>food</u> or <u>blood</u>.

5) They're mainly <u>protein-digesting</u> enzymes (<u>proteases</u>) and <u>fat-digesting</u> enzymes (<u>lipases</u>).

| Stain | Sources of stain | Enzymes | Product |
|---|---|---|---|
| Protein | Blood, grass | Proteases | Amino acids |
| Lipid (fats) | Butter, oil | Lipases | Fatty acids and glycerol |

The <u>products</u> of these enzyme-controlled reactions are <u>soluble in water</u> and so can be easily washed out of clothes.

6) Biological detergents are also <u>more effective</u> at working at <u>low temperatures</u> (e.g. 30 °C) than other types of detergents.

## Enzymes Are Used to Change Foods in Industry

Enzymes are used to <u>treat</u> some foods during <u>manufacturing</u>:

1) The <u>proteins</u> in some <u>baby foods</u> are 'pre-digested' using protein-digesting enzymes (<u>proteases</u>), so they're easier for the baby to digest.

2) Carbohydrate-digesting enzymes (<u>carbohydrases</u>) can be used to turn <u>starch syrup</u> (yuk) into <u>sugar syrup</u> (yum).

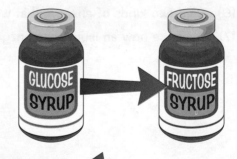

3) <u>Glucose syrup</u> can be turned into <u>fructose syrup</u> using an <u>isomerase</u> enzyme. Fructose is <u>sweeter</u>, so you can get the same level of sweetness using <u>less sugar</u>. This helps make <u>slimming foods and drinks</u> sweeter without adding too many calories.

## There's a lot to learn — but don't be deterred gents...
And there you have it — enzymes in all their glory. They're really <u>picky</u> — even tiny little changes in pH or temperature will stop them working at maximum efficiency. They only catalyse <u>one reaction</u> as well, so you need to use a different one for each reaction. Temperamental little things...

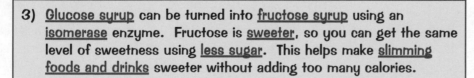

# Revision Summary for Section Three

Well, that was quite a short section. But just to be on the safe side, we'd better have a few questions to make sure you were awake for it. Use these to find out what you know — and what you don't. Then look back and learn the bits you don't know. Then try the questions again, and again...

1) What are carbohydrates made up of?

2) What type of molecule is made up of one molecule of glycerol and three fatty acid molecules?

3) What type of molecule is made up of amino acids?

4) Describe four functions of proteins in living cells.

5) Give a definition of a catalyst.

6) Explain why an enzyme-catalysed reaction stops when the reaction mixture is heated above a certain temperature.

7) What is meant by the 'optimum pH' of an enzyme?

8) What is the job of digestive enzymes?

9) In which three places in the body is amylase produced?

10) Where does lipase work?

11) Where in the body is bile:
    a) produced?
    b) stored?
    c) used?

12) What does bile do to fats? How does this help digestion?

13) Explain why the stomach produces hydrochloric acid.

14) Describe the function(s) of the:
    a) salivary glands
    b) pancreas
    c) gall bladder

15) What is absorbed from
    a) the small intestine?
    b) the large intestine?

16) Give two kinds of enzyme that would be useful in a biological washing powder.

17) Describe how an isomerase enzyme is used in the production of slimming foods.

*Section Three — Enzymes and Digestion*

# The Nervous System

The nervous system allows you to react to what goes on around you — you'd find life tough without it.

## Sense Organs Detect Stimuli

A <u>stimulus</u> is a <u>change in your environment</u> which you may need to react to (e.g. a grizzly bear looking hungrily at you). You need to be constantly monitoring what's going on so you can respond if you need to.

1) You have five different <u>sense organs</u> — eyes, ears, nose, tongue and skin.

2) They all contain different <u>receptors</u>. Receptors are groups of cells which are <u>sensitive</u> to <u>stimuli</u> (changes in the environment). They change <u>stimulus energy</u> (e.g. light energy) into <u>electrical impulses</u>.

3) A stimulus can be <u>light</u>, <u>sound</u>, <u>touch</u>, <u>pressure</u>, <u>pain</u>, <u>chemical</u>, or a change in <u>position</u> or <u>temperature</u>.

> Sense organs and receptors — don't get them mixed up. E.g. the eye is a sense organ — it contains light receptors.

The <u>Five Sense Organs</u> and the <u>receptors</u> that each contains:

**1) Eyes**  <u>Light</u> receptors — sensitive to <u>light</u>. These cells have a nucleus, cytoplasm and cell membrane (just like most animal cells).

**2) Ears**  <u>Sound</u> receptors — sensitive to <u>sound</u>. Also, "<u>balance</u>" receptors — sensitive to <u>changes in position</u>.

**3) Nose**  <u>Smell</u> receptors — sensitive to <u>chemical</u> stimuli.

**4) Tongue**  <u>Taste</u> receptors — sensitive to bitter, salt, sweet and sour, plus the taste of savoury things like monosodium glutamate (MSG) — <u>chemical</u> stimuli.

**5) Skin**  Sensitive to <u>touch</u>, <u>pressure</u>, <u>pain</u> and <u>temperature change</u>.

## The Central Nervous System Coordinates a Response

1) <u>The central nervous system</u> (CNS) consists of <u>the brain</u> and <u>spinal cord</u> only. These <u>coordination centres</u> are where the information from receptors in the sense organs is <u>sent</u> to, and where responses are <u>coordinated</u>.

2) <u>Neurones</u> (nerve cells) <u>transmit the information</u> (as <u>electrical impulses</u>) very quickly to and from the CNS.

3) "<u>Instructions</u>" from the CNS are sent to the <u>effectors</u> (<u>muscles and glands</u>), which respond accordingly.

### Sensory Neurones

The <u>nerve cells</u> that carry signals as <u>electrical impulses</u> from the <u>receptors</u> in the sense organs to the <u>central nervous system</u>.

### Relay Neurones

The <u>nerve cells</u> that carry signals from <u>sensory neurones</u> to <u>motor neurones</u>.

### Motor Neurones

The <u>nerve cells</u> that carry signals from the <u>central nervous system</u> to the <u>effector</u> muscles or glands.

### Effectors

Muscles and glands are known as <u>effectors</u> — they respond in different ways. <u>Muscles contract</u> in response to a nervous impulse, whereas <u>glands secrete chemicals</u> (<u>hormones</u>) (see page 46).

## Control Systems

Automatic <u>control systems</u> inside the body help to <u>keep conditions constant</u> by <u>responding</u> to <u>changes</u> (stimuli). Control systems are formed of <u>receptors</u>, <u>coordination centres</u> and <u>effectors</u>:

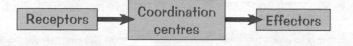

Receptors → Coordination centres → Effectors

## This page will get your receptors going...

...no, don't lick it. Listen up. Exams aren't just a test of what you know — they're also a test of how well you can <u>apply</u> what you know. For instance, you might have to take what you know about a <u>human</u> and apply it to a <u>horse</u> (easy... sound receptors in its ears, light receptors in its eyes, etc.) Thinking in an exam... gosh.

# Reflexes

Neurones transmit information <u>very quickly</u> to and from the brain, and your brain <u>quickly decides</u> how to respond to a stimulus. But <u>reflexes</u> are even quicker...

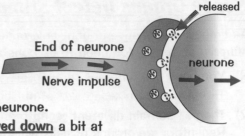

## Synapses Connect Neurones

1) The <u>connection</u> between <u>two neurones</u> is called a <u>synapse</u>.

2) The nerve signal is transferred by <u>chemicals</u> which <u>diffuse</u> (move) across the gap.

3) These chemicals then set off a <u>new electrical signal</u> in the <u>next</u> neurone.

4) The <u>transmission</u> of a nervous <u>impulse</u> is <u>very fast</u>, but it is <u>slowed down</u> a bit at the synapse because the <u>diffusion</u> of chemicals across the gap takes <u>time</u>.

## Reflexes Help Prevent Injury

1) <u>Reflexes</u> are <u>automatic</u>, <u>rapid</u> responses to certain stimuli — they can reduce the chances of being injured.

2) For example, if someone shines a <u>bright light</u> in your eyes, your <u>pupils</u> automatically get smaller so that less light gets into the eye — this stops it getting <u>damaged</u>.

3) Or if you get a shock, your body releases the <u>hormone</u> adrenaline automatically — it doesn't wait for you to <u>decide</u> that you're shocked.

4) The passage of information in a reflex (from receptor to effector) is called a <u>reflex arc</u>.

## The Reflex Arc Goes Through the Central Nervous System

1) The neurones in reflex arcs go through the <u>spinal cord</u> or through an <u>unconscious part of the brain</u>.

2) When a <u>stimulus</u> (e.g. a bee sting) is detected by receptors, <u>impulses</u> are sent along a <u>sensory neurone</u> to the CNS.

3) When the impulses reach a <u>synapse</u> between the sensory neurone and a relay neurone, they trigger chemicals to be released (see above). These chemicals cause impulses to be sent along the <u>relay neurone</u>.

4) When the impulses reach a <u>synapse</u> between the relay neurone and a motor neurone, the same thing happens. Chemicals are released and cause impulses to be sent along the <u>motor neurone</u>.

5) The impulses then travel along the motor neurone to the <u>effector</u> (in this example it's a muscle, but it could be a gland which would react by releasing chemicals).

6) The <u>muscle</u> then <u>contracts</u> and moves your hand away from the bee.

7) Because you don't have to think about the response (which takes time) it's <u>quicker</u> than normal responses.

5. Impulses travel along a motor neurone, via a synapse.

4. Impulses are passed along a relay neurone, via a synapse.

6. When impulses reach muscle, it contracts.

3. Impulses travel along the sensory neurone.

2. Stimulation of the pain receptor.

1. Cheeky bee stings finger.

<u>Behaviours</u> (e.g. waving) take a similar pathway to reflexes. The pathway goes through <u>conscious</u> parts of the <u>brain</u> instead of the <u>unconscious</u> parts though. In the exam, you could be asked to <u>analyse</u> an example of <u>behaviour</u> or a <u>reflex arc</u> in terms of the <u>stimulus</u>, <u>receptor</u>, <u>coordinator</u>, <u>effector</u> and <u>response</u>, as shown here.

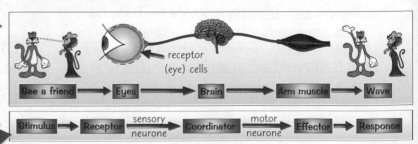

See a friend → Eyes → Brain → Arm muscle → Wave

receptor (eye) cells

Stimulus → Receptor → (sensory neurone) → Coordinator → (motor neurone) → Effector → Response

## Don't get all twitchy — just learn it...

Reflexes bypass your conscious brain completely when a quick response is essential — your body just gets on with things. Right, time to get learning this lot. Bet you wish revision was an automatic response...

# The Brain

Scientists know a bit about the <u>brain</u> but <u>not as much</u> as they'd like. Their knowledge is improving with the invention of new <u>gadgetry</u> that helps them study the brain. Read on, it's pretty amazing stuff.

## The Brain is Responsible for Complex Behaviours

1) Along with the spinal cord, the brain is part of the <u>central nervous system</u>.

2) It's made up of <u>billions</u> of <u>interconnected neurones</u> (neurones that are connected together).

3) The brain is in charge of all of our <u>complex behaviours</u>. It controls and coordinates everything you do — running, breathing, sleeping, remembering where you left your gym kit...

4) We know that <u>different regions</u> of the brain carry out <u>different functions</u>:

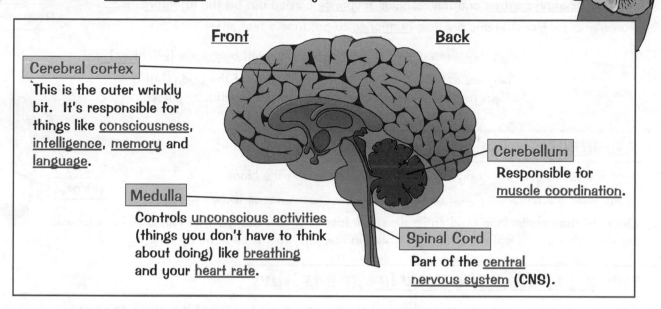

Front        Back

**Cerebral cortex**
This is the outer wrinkly bit. It's responsible for things like <u>consciousness</u>, <u>intelligence</u>, <u>memory</u> and <u>language</u>.

**Cerebellum**
Responsible for <u>muscle coordination</u>.

**Medulla**
Controls <u>unconscious activities</u> (things you don't have to think about doing) like <u>breathing</u> and your <u>heart rate</u>.

**Spinal Cord**
Part of the <u>central nervous system</u> (CNS).

## Scientists Use a Range of Methods to Study the Brain

Scientists use a few different methods to study the brain and figure out <u>which bits do what</u>:

① **Studying patients with brain damage** — If a <u>small</u> part of the brain has been <u>damaged</u> the <u>effect</u> this has on the patient can tell you a lot about what the damaged part of the brain does. E.g. if an area at the back of the brain was damaged by a stroke and the patient went <u>blind</u> you know that that area has something to do with <u>vision</u>.

② **Electrically stimulating the brain** — The brain can be <u>stimulated electrically</u> by pushing a tiny <u>electrode</u> into the tissue and giving it a small zap of electricity. By observing what stimulating <u>different parts</u> of the brain does, it's possible to get an idea of what those parts do. E.g. when a certain part of the brain (know as the <u>motor area</u>) is stimulated, it causes <u>muscle contraction</u> and <u>movement</u>.

③ **MRI Scans** — A <u>magnetic resonance imaging (MRI) scanner</u> is a big fancy tube-like machine that can produce a very <u>detailed picture</u> of the brain's structures. Scientists use it to find out what areas of the brain are <u>active</u> when people are doing things like listening to music or trying to recall a memory.

## A whole page dedicated to that squidgy thing in your head...

...lucky you. But actually it's really fascinating stuff. As <u>technology improves</u>, neuroscientists (scientists that study the brain) are learning more and more about what goes on up there. This knowledge can be used to help understand <u>how our minds work</u>, develop <u>treatments for diseases</u>, and to <u>help people</u> who have had brain injuries.

# Homeostasis

Homeostasis is a fancy word, but all it really means is trying to maintain a "constant internal environment".

## Your Body Needs Some Things to Be Kept Constant

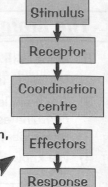

1) To keep all your cells working properly, certain things must be kept at the right level — not too high, and not too low.

2) Bodily levels that need to be controlled include:
   - Ion content
   - Water content
   - Temperature
   - Sugar content (blood glucose level)

3) These things are kept constant by automatic control systems. Like in the nervous system, this involves the detection of a stimulus by receptors, processing of this information by the coordination centres and the resulting response carried out by the effectors.

4) Automatic control systems can use hormones to produce a response:

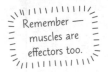
Remember — muscles are effectors too.

   - Hormones are chemical substances secreted by glands (effectors).
   - They are carried in the blood to other parts of the body, but only affect particular cells (called target cells) in particular places.

```
Stimulus
   ↓
Receptor
   ↓
Coordination
   centre
   ↓
Effectors
   ↓
Response
```

## Ion Content is Regulated by the Kidneys

1) Ions are taken into the body in food, then absorbed into the blood.

2) If the food contains too much of an ion then the excess needs to be removed.

3) Some of the excess ions (and some urea) are lost in sweat, but the rest needs to be removed by the kidneys and got rid of in urine (see next page). This is all done by an automatic control system.

Kidneys

## Water is Lost from the Body in Various Ways

1) The body also needs to constantly balance the water coming in against the water going out.

2) Water is taken into the body as food and drink and is lost from the body in these ways:
   - through the SKIN as SWEAT...
   - via the LUNGS in BREATH...
   - via the kidneys as URINE.

Some water is also lost in faeces.

3) Hormones control body water content (see p. 48) and the brain is the coordination centre.

## Body Temperature is Controlled by the Brain

1) All enzymes work best at a certain temperature. The enzymes within the human body work best at about 37 °C — and so this is the temperature your body tries to maintain (see p. 50).

2) A part of the brain acts as your own personal thermostat. It's sensitive to the blood temperature in the brain, and it receives messages from receptors in the skin that provide information about skin temperature.

## Blood Sugar Level Needs to Be Controlled Too

1) Eating foods containing carbohydrate puts glucose into the blood from the gut.

2) The normal metabolism of cells removes glucose from the blood.

3) A hormone called insulin helps to maintain the right level of glucose in your blood, so your cells get a constant supply of energy (see p. 51).

4) The pancreas acts as the coordination centre in the control of blood glucose.

## My sister never goes out — she's got homeostasis...

There's loads more on homeostasis coming up on the next few pages. Brace yourself...

# The Liver and Kidneys

Our cells produce <u>waste products</u> which the body needs to <u>excrete</u> (get rid of). The <u>liver</u> breaks down these waste products into less harmful substances and then the <u>kidneys</u> kick them out in the <u>urine</u>. Job well done.

## The Liver is Responsible for Deamination and Detoxification

1) The <u>liver</u> gets rid of the <u>excess amino acids</u> produced when we eat and digest <u>protein</u>. Large amounts of amino acids can be <u>damaging</u> if they stay in the body, so they must be <u>broken down</u> and <u>excreted</u>.

2) The liver breaks down <u>amino acids</u> into <u>ammonia</u> by a process called <u>deamination</u>.

3) The <u>ammonia</u> is converted into <u>urea</u>. Some of this urea is lost in the <u>sweat</u>, but most is removed from the body in the <u>urine</u> by the <u>kidneys</u> (see below).

4) The liver breaks down other <u>harmful substances</u> too (alcohol, drugs and unwanted hormones). It breaks them into <u>less harmful</u> substances that are <u>excreted</u> in the urine. This process is called <u>detoxification</u>.

5) <u>Old blood cells</u> are also removed from the blood in the liver. Red blood cells contain lots of <u>iron</u>, so the blood cells are broken down and the iron is <u>stored</u> for use in the body.

## The Kidneys Filter the Blood to Produce Urine

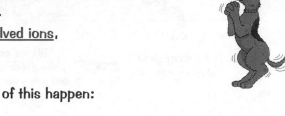

The <u>kidneys</u> are pretty important. Here's what they do:

1) <u>Filter</u> the blood (to remove unwanted or excess products).

2) <u>Reabsorb products</u> that are <u>needed</u>: all <u>glucose</u>, any <u>dissolved ions</u>, and any <u>water</u> needed by the body.

3) <u>Release urea</u>, <u>excess ions</u> and <u>excess water</u> as <u>urine</u>.

<u>Nephrons</u> are the <u>filtration units</u> in the kidneys which make all of this happen:

### 1) Ultrafiltration:

1) A <u>high pressure</u> is built up which squeezes <u>water</u>, <u>urea</u>, <u>ions</u> and <u>sugar</u> out of the blood and into the <u>Bowman's capsule</u> (see bottom diagram).

2) The membranes between the blood vessels and the Bowman's capsule act like <u>filters</u>, so <u>big</u> molecules like <u>proteins</u> and <u>blood cells</u> are <u>not</u> squeezed out. They stay in the blood.

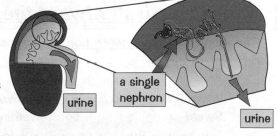

a single nephron

urine

urine

### 2) Reabsorption:

As the liquid flows along the nephron, <u>useful</u> substances are <u>reabsorbed</u> back into the blood:

1) <u>All</u> the <u>sugar</u> is reabsorbed. This involves the process of <u>active transport</u> against the concentration gradient.

2) <u>Sufficient ions</u> are reabsorbed. Excess ions are not. <u>Active transport</u> is needed.

3) <u>Sufficient water</u> is reabsorbed.

### 3) Release of wastes:

The remaining substances (including <u>urea</u>) continue out of the <u>nephron</u>, into the ureter and down to the <u>bladder</u> as <u>urine</u>.

## Enlarged View of a Single Nephron

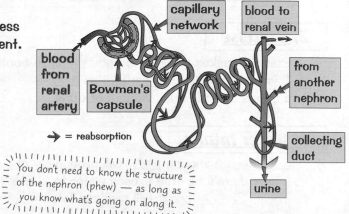

capillary network

blood to renal vein

blood from renal artery

Bowman's capsule

from another nephron

→ = reabsorption

collecting duct

urine

You don't need to know the structure of the nephron (phew) — as long as you know what's going on along it.

## Don't try to kid-me that you know it all — learn it properly...

The kidneys are pretty <u>complicated</u> organs as you can see. Luckily you don't have to learn all the <u>ins and outs</u> of the diagram — but you do have to make sure you know <u>exactly</u> what the <u>liver</u> and the <u>kidneys</u> do.

*Section Four — Nerves and Homeostasis*

# Controlling Water Content

Lots of things affect the water content of the blood.  Luckily there's an <u>automatic control system</u> in place to keep things nice and <u>steady</u>.  Enough talk, lets get cracking — hope you've been to the loo...

## Water Content is Controlled by the Kidneys

It's important to keep a <u>constant concentration</u> of <u>water molecules</u> in the <u>blood plasma</u>.  This prevents too much water moving into or out of the tissues by <u>osmosis</u>.  It also keeps the <u>blood pressure constant</u>.

1)  The amount of water reabsorbed in the <u>kidney nephrons</u> (see previous page) is <u>controlled</u> by a hormone called <u>anti-diuretic hormone</u> (ADH).  ADH makes the nephrons more <u>permeable</u> so that more water is reabsorbed back into the blood.

2)  The brain <u>monitors the water content of the blood</u> and instructs the <u>pituitary gland</u> to release <u>ADH</u> into the blood according to how much is needed:

- If the <u>water content</u> of the <u>blood</u> is <u>too low</u>, ADH is <u>released</u> into the blood. The kidneys <u>reabsorb more water</u> and a <u>more concentrated urine</u> is produced.

- If the <u>water content</u> of the <u>blood</u> is <u>too high</u>, <u>less ADH</u> is <u>released</u> into the blood. The kidneys <u>reabsorb less water</u> and a <u>more dilute urine</u> is produced.

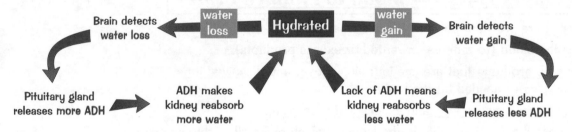

## Your Urine isn't Always the Same

The <u>amount</u> and <u>concentration</u> of <u>urine</u> is controlled by <u>ADH</u>.  It depends on three main things:

### 1) Heat

When it's <u>hot</u> you <u>sweat</u> (which evaporates, cooling down the skin). Sweat <u>contains water</u>, so... sweating causes <u>water loss</u>.
This causes the <u>release of ADH</u> into the <u>blood</u> so that the <u>kidneys</u> will <u>reabsorb more water</u>.  This leaves only a small amount of excess water that needs to be got rid of — so only a small amount of quite <u>concentrated urine</u> will be <u>produced</u>.

### 2) Exercise

Exercise makes you <u>hot</u>, so you <u>sweat</u> to cool down.
This produces the <u>same effect</u> as <u>heat</u> —
a concentrated, small volume of urine.

### 3) Water Intake

<u>Not drinking</u> enough <u>water</u> will produce <u>concentrated urine</u> (since there'll be little excess water to 'dilute' the other wastes).
<u>Drinking lots of water</u> will produce lots of <u>dilute urine</u>.

## Simon says touch urea... actually don't...

...it's a little bit gross.  Diseased kidneys can't control the <u>water content</u> of the <u>blood</u>, so kidney failure patients often have <u>high blood pressure</u>.  This excess water is removed during dialysis (see next page).

# Kidney Failure

If someone's kidneys stop working, there are basically two treatments — regular dialysis or a transplant.

## The Kidneys Remove Waste Substances from the Blood

1) If the kidneys don't work properly, waste substances build up in the blood and you lose your ability to control the levels of ions and water in your body. Eventually, this results in death.

2) People with kidney failure can be kept alive by having dialysis treatment — where machines do the job of the kidneys. Or they can have a kidney transplant.

*The kidneys are incredibly important — if they don't work as they should, you can get problems in the heart, bones, nervous system, stomach, mouth, etc.*

## Dialysis Machines Filter the Blood

1) Dialysis has to be done regularly to keep the concentrations of dissolved substances in the blood at normal levels, and to remove waste substances.

2) In a dialysis machine the person's blood flows between partially permeable membranes, surrounded by dialysis fluid. It's permeable to things like ions and waste substances, but not big molecules like proteins (just like the membranes in the kidney).

dialysis fluid out

partially permeable membrane

dialysis fluid in

waste products diffuse out into dialysis fluid

from person

back to person

3) The dialysis fluid has the same concentration of dissolved ions and glucose as healthy blood.

4) This means that useful dissolved ions and glucose won't be lost from the blood during dialysis.

5) Only waste substances (such as urea) and excess ions and water diffuse across the barrier.

6) Many patients with kidney failure have to have a dialysis session three times a week. Each session takes 3-4 hours — not much fun.

7) Plus, dialysis may cause blood clots or infections.

8) Being on a dialysis machine is not a pleasant experience and it is expensive for the NHS to run.

9) However, dialysis can buy a patient with kidney failure valuable time until a donor organ is found.

## Kidney Transplants are a Cure, but Donor Organs can be Rejected

1) At the moment, the only cure for kidney failure is to have a kidney transplant.

2) Healthy kidneys are usually transplanted from people who have died suddenly.

3) The person who died has to be on the organ donor register or carry a donor card (provided their relatives agree too).

4) Kidneys can also be transplanted from people who are still alive (as we all have two of them) but there is a small risk to the person donating the kidney.

5) There is also a risk that the donor kidney can be rejected by the patient's immune system (see page 34 for more). The patient is treated with drugs to prevent this but it can still happen.

6) Transplants are cheaper (in the long run) than dialysis and they can put an end to the hours patients have to spend on dialysis, but there are long waiting lists for kidneys.

## Dialysis or transplant? Both have their downsides...

In the exam, you could be asked to evaluate the advantages and disadvantages of treating kidney failure in different ways. Make sure you know a few positives and few negatives for both dialysis and organ transplantation.

# Controlling Body Temperature

If you've ever wondered why you get all <u>sweaty</u> when running for the bus, or why you <u>shiver</u> when your dad refuses to put the heating on, don't worry — it's just your body's way of keeping your <u>temperature constant</u>.

## Body Temperature Must Be Carefully Controlled

As you know, the enzymes within the <u>human body</u> work best at about <u>37 °C</u> (see page 38).
If the body gets too hot or too cold, the enzymes <u>won't work properly</u> and some really important <u>reactions</u> could be <u>disrupted</u>. In extreme cases, this can even lead to <u>death</u>.

There is a <u>thermoregulatory centre</u> in the <u>brain</u> which acts as your own <u>personal thermostat</u>. It contains <u>receptors</u> that are sensitive to the temperature of the <u>blood</u> flowing through the brain.
The thermoregulatory centre also receives impulses from receptors in the <u>skin</u>, giving info about <u>skin temperature</u>.

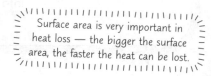

If you're getting too hot or too cold, your body can <u>respond</u> to try and cool you down or warm you up:

### When you're TOO HOT:

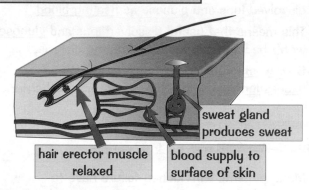

hair erector muscle relaxed

sweat gland produces sweat

blood supply to surface of skin

1) <u>Hairs</u> lie flat.
2) <u>Sweat</u> is produced by sweat glands and <u>evaporates</u> from the skin, which removes heat.
3) The <u>blood vessels</u> supplying the skin capillaries <u>dilate</u> so more blood flows close to the surface of the skin.
4) The vessels now have a <u>larger surface area</u>, which means more heat can be lost from the blood to the environment by <u>radiation</u>.

Surface area is very important in heat loss — the bigger the surface area, the faster the heat can be lost.

### When you're TOO COLD:

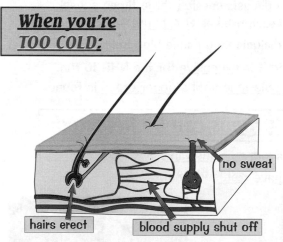

hairs erect

no sweat

blood supply shut off

1) <u>Hairs</u> stand up to trap an <u>insulating layer</u> of <u>air</u>.
2) <u>No sweat</u> is produced.
3) Blood vessels supplying skin capillaries <u>constrict</u> to <u>reduce</u> the skin's blood supply.
4) The <u>constriction</u> of the blood vessels reduces the <u>surface area</u> of the vessels. This means less heat is lost by <u>radiation</u>.
5) When you're <u>cold</u> you <u>shiver</u> too (your muscles contract automatically). This needs <u>respiration</u>, which releases some <u>energy</u> to <u>warm</u> the body.

## Water Lost Through Sweating Needs to be Replaced

1) The <u>sweat</u> you produce to <u>cool</u> you down <u>contains water</u>, so... sweating causes <u>water loss</u>.
2) More water is lost when it's <u>hot</u>, or when you're <u>exercising</u> because you <u>sweat more</u>.
3) This fluid needs to be <u>replaced</u> by drinking <u>water</u> or through eating <u>food</u> (which contains water) to help <u>balance</u> the loss.

## Shiver me timbers — it's a wee bit nippy in here...

People who are exposed to extreme cold for long periods of time without protection can get <u>frostbite</u> — the blood supply to the fingers and toes is cut off to conserve heat (but this kills the cells, and they go black)... yuk.

# Controlling Blood Glucose

Blood glucose is also controlled as part of homeostasis. Insulin and glucagon are the two hormones involved.

## Insulin and Glucagon Control Blood Glucose Level

1) Eating foods containing carbohydrate puts glucose (a type of sugar) into the blood from the small intestine.

2) The normal metabolism of cells removes glucose from the blood.

3) Vigorous exercise removes much more glucose from the blood.

4) Excess glucose can be stored as glycogen in the liver and in the muscles.

5) When these stores are full then the excess glucose is stored as lipid (fat) in the tissues.

6) The level of glucose in the blood must be kept steady. Changes in blood glucose are monitored and controlled by the pancreas, using the hormones insulin and glucagon, as shown:

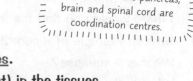
Remember — the pancreas, brain and spinal cord are coordination centres.

**Blood glucose level TOO HIGH — INSULIN is ADDED**

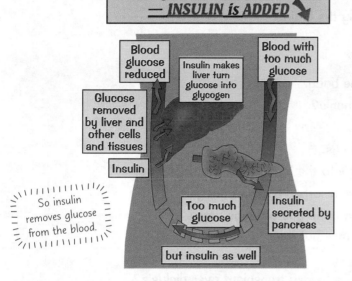

So insulin removes glucose from the blood.

**Blood glucose level TOO LOW — GLUCAGON is ADDED**

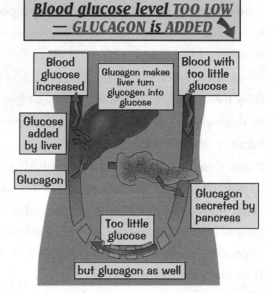

## Having Diabetes Means You Can't Control Your Blood Sugar Level

Diabetes is a condition that affects your ability to control your blood sugar level. There are two types:

1) Type 1 diabetes is where the pancreas produces little or no insulin. This means a person's blood glucose level can rise to a level that can kill them. People with Type 1 diabetes can partly control the condition by having a carefully controlled diet and by taking regular exercise (see below). They also need to inject insulin, usually several times a day and most likely at mealtimes. This will make the liver remove the glucose as soon as it enters the blood from the gut, when the food is being digested. This stops the level of glucose in the blood from getting too high and is a very effective treatment. The amount of insulin that needs to be injected depends on the person's diet and how active they are.

2) Type 2 diabetes is where a person becomes resistant to their own insulin (they still produce insulin, but their body's cells don't respond properly to the hormone). This can also cause a person's blood sugar level to rise to a dangerous level. Being overweight can increase your chance of developing Type 2 diabetes, as obesity is a major risk factor in the development of the disease. Type 2 diabetes is usually just controlled by avoiding foods rich in simple carbohydrates, i.e. sugars (which cause glucose levels to rise rapidly). Exercise also helps keep a person's blood glucose level down as the increased metabolism of cells during exercise removes more glucose from the blood. There are also some drugs available which improve the way that the body's cells respond to insulin.

## My blood sugar feels low after all that — pass the biscuits...

This stuff can seem a bit confusing at first, but if you learn those two diagrams, it'll all start to get a lot easier. Don't forget that there are two types of diabetes — and different ways of controlling them.

# Revision Summary for Section Four

Congratulations, you've made it to the end of this section. I reckon that section wasn't too bad, there's some pretty interesting stuff there — the brain and nervous system, kidney dialysis and organ transplant, controlling blood sugar level, sweat and urine... lovely. What more could you want? Actually, I know what more you could want, some questions to make sure you know it all.

1) Where would you find the following receptors in a dog: a) smell b) taste c) light d) pressure e) sound?
2) Give an example of a coordination centre found in the body.
3) What is a synapse?
4) What is the purpose of a reflex action?
5) Describe the pathway of a reflex arc from stimulus to response.
6) Which part of the brain is responsible for unconscious activities such as breathing?
7) Give one thing the cerebral cortex is responsible for.
8) Give three methods used by scientists to study the brain.
9) What are hormones?
10) What are hormones secreted by?
11) Give three ways in which water is lost from the body.
12) In deamination, what is broken down into ammonia?
13) What is detoxification?
14) Name three things that are reabsorbed by kidneys.
15) Explain why sugar doesn't simply diffuse back into the blood from the nephrons.
16) What hormone controls the amount of water reabsorbed by the kidneys?
17) Describe how the amount and concentration of urine you produce varies depending on how much exercise you do and how hot it is.
18) How does kidney dialysis work?
19) What are the advantages and disadvantages of a kidney transplant over dialysis?
20) Where is the thermoregulatory centre located?
21) How does the dilation of the blood vessels supplying the skin capillaries increase heat loss?
22) Write down three things that the body can do to reduce heat loss if it gets too cold.
23) Where is excess glucose stored in the body?
24) Describe what happens when your blood glucose level is too high.
25) What effect does the hormone glucagon have on blood glucose level?
26) What causes Type 1 diabetes? How is Type 1 diabetes be controlled?
27) What causes Type 2 diabetes?
28) Which type of diabetes is associated with obesity?
29) Give three ways in which Type 2 diabetes can be controlled.

# Fighting Disease

Microorganisms that enter the body and cause disease are called pathogens. Pathogens cause infectious diseases — diseases that can easily spread.

## There Are Two Main Types of Pathogen: Bacteria and Viruses

### 1. Bacteria Are Very Small Living Cells

1) Bacteria are very small cells (about 1/100th the size of your body cells), which can reproduce rapidly inside your body.

2) They make you feel ill by doing two things: a) damaging your cells, b) producing toxins (poisons).

### 2. Viruses Are Not Cells — They're Much Smaller

1) Viruses are not cells. They're tiny, about 1/100th the size of a bacterium.

2) They replicate themselves by invading your cells and using the cells' machinery to produce many copies of themselves. The cell will usually then burst, releasing all the new viruses.

3) This cell damage is what makes you feel ill.

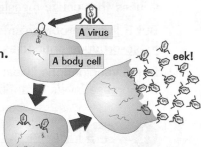

A virus

A body cell

eek!

## Your Body Has a Pretty Sophisticated Defence System

1) Your skin, plus hairs and mucus in your respiratory tract (breathing pipework), stop a lot of nasties getting inside your body.

2) And to try and prevent microorganisms getting into the body through cuts, small fragments of cells (called platelets) help blood clot quickly to seal wounds. If the blood contains low numbers of platelets then it will clot more slowly.

3) But if something does make it through, your immune system kicks in. The most important part is the white blood cells. They travel around in your blood and crawl into every part of you, constantly patrolling for microbes. When they come across an invading microbe they have three lines of attack.

### 1. Consuming Them

White blood cells can engulf foreign cells and digest them.

microbes

White Blood Cell

### 2. Producing Antibodies

1) Every invading cell has unique molecules (called antigens) on its surface.

2) When your white blood cells come across a foreign antigen (i.e. one they don't recognise), they will start to produce proteins called antibodies to lock onto and kill the invading cells. The antibodies produced are specific to that type of antigen — they won't lock on to any others.

3) Antibodies are then produced rapidly and carried around the body to kill all similar bacteria or viruses.

4) If the person is infected with the same pathogen again the white blood cells will rapidly produce the antibodies to kill it — the person is naturally immune to that pathogen and won't get ill.

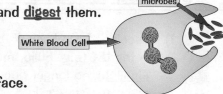

New microbe

Antibodies produced

White blood cell

New microbes attacked by new antibodies

### 3. Producing Antitoxins

These counteract toxins produced by the invading bacteria.

## Fight disease — blow your nose with boxing gloves...

If you have a low level of white blood cells, you'll be more susceptible to infections. E.g. HIV/AIDS attacks a person's white blood cells and weakens their immune system, making it easier for other pathogens to invade.

# Fighting Disease — Vaccination

Vaccinations have changed the way we fight disease. We don't always have to deal with the problem once it's happened — we can prevent it happening in the first place.

## Vaccination — Protects from Future Infections

1) When you're infected with a new microorganism, it takes your white blood cells a few days to learn how to deal with it. But by that time, you can be pretty ill.

2) Vaccinations involve injecting small amounts of dead or inactive microorganisms. These carry antigens, which cause your body to produce antibodies to attack them — even though the microorganism is harmless (since it's dead or inactive). For example, the MMR vaccine contains weakened versions of the viruses that cause measles, mumps and rubella (German measles) all in one vaccine.

3) But if live microorganisms of the same type appear after that, the white blood cells can rapidly mass-produce antibodies to kill off the pathogen. Cool.

4) Some vaccinations "wear off" over time. So booster injections may need to be given to increase levels of antibodies again.

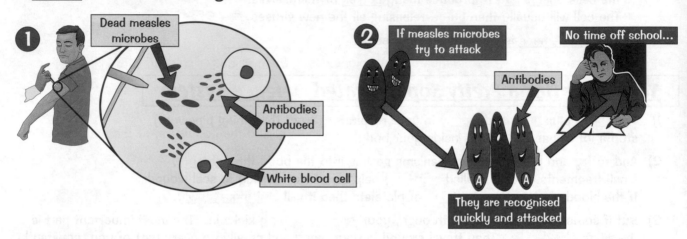

Dead measles microbes

Antibodies produced

White blood cell

If measles microbes try to attack

Antibodies

No time off school...

They are recognised quickly and attacked

## There are Pros and Cons of Vaccination

Vaccination is sometimes called immunisation.

**PROS**

1) Vaccines have helped control lots of infectious diseases that were once common in the UK (e.g. polio, measles, whooping cough, rubella, mumps, tetanus...). Smallpox no longer occurs at all, and polio infections have fallen by 99%.

2) Big outbreaks of disease — called epidemics — can be prevented if a large percentage of the population is vaccinated. That way, even the people who aren't vaccinated are unlikely to catch the disease because there are fewer people able to pass it on. But if a significant number of people aren't vaccinated, the disease can spread quickly through them and lots of people will be ill at the same time.

**CONS**

1) Vaccines don't always work — sometimes they don't give you immunity.

2) You can sometimes have a bad reaction to a vaccine (e.g. swelling, or maybe something more serious like a fever or seizures). But bad reactions are very rare.

## Prevention is better than cure...

Deciding whether to have a vaccination means balancing risks — the risk of catching the disease if you don't have a vaccine, against the risk of having a bad reaction if you do. As always, you need to look at the evidence. For example, if you get measles (the disease), there's about a 1 in 15 chance that you'll get complications (e.g. pneumonia) — and about 1 in 500 people who get measles actually die. However, the number of people who have a problem with the vaccine is more like 1 in 1 000 000.

# Fighting Disease — Drugs

*...a biscuit, nurse? Thanks very much. Sorry, couldn't face that last page — I'm squeamish about needles.\**

## Some Drugs Just Relieve Symptoms — Others Cure the Problem

1) <u>Painkillers</u> (e.g. aspirin) are drugs that relieve pain (no, really). However, they don't actually tackle the <u>cause</u> of the disease (the pathogens), they just help to reduce the <u>symptoms</u>.

2) Other drugs do a similar kind of thing — reduce the <u>symptoms</u> without tackling the underlying <u>cause</u>. For example, lots of "cold remedies" don't actually <u>cure</u> colds.

3) <u>Antibiotics</u> (e.g. penicillin) work differently — they actually <u>kill</u> (or prevent the growth of) the bacteria causing the problem without killing your own body cells. <u>Different antibiotics</u> kill <u>different types</u> of bacteria, so it's important to be treated with the <u>right one</u>.

4) But antibiotics <u>don't destroy viruses</u> (e.g. <u>flu</u> or <u>cold</u> viruses). Viruses reproduce <u>using your own body cells</u>, which makes it very difficult to develop drugs that destroy just the virus without killing the body's cells.

## Bacteria Can Become Resistant to Antibiotics

1) Bacteria can <u>mutate</u> — sometimes the mutations cause them to be <u>resistant</u> to (not killed by) an <u>antibiotic</u>.

2) If you have an <u>infection</u>, some of the bacteria might be <u>resistant</u> to antibiotics.

3) This means that when you <u>treat</u> the infection, only the <u>non-resistant</u> strains of bacteria will be <u>killed</u>.

4) The individual <u>resistant</u> bacteria will <u>survive</u> and <u>reproduce</u>, and the population of the resistant strain will <u>increase</u>. This is an example of natural selection (see page 91).

5) Vaccinations might <u>no longer work</u> against this <u>resistant strain</u>, and it could cause a <u>serious infection</u> that <u>can't</u> be treated by antibiotics. E.g. <u>MRSA</u> (methicillin-resistant *Staphylococcus aureus*) causes serious wound infections and is resistant to the powerful antibiotic <u>methicillin</u>.

6) The new resistant strain of bacteria could <u>spread rapidly</u> in a population of people because they are <u>not immune</u> to it and there is <u>no effective treatment</u>. It could even cause an <u>epidemic</u> — a big outbreak of disease.

7) To <u>slow down</u> the <u>rate</u> of development of <u>resistant strains</u>, it's important for doctors to <u>avoid over-prescribing</u> antibiotics and avoid using them <u>inappropriately</u>. E.g. you <u>shouldn't</u> get them for a <u>sore throat</u>, only for something more serious.

## Antibiotic Resistance is Becoming More Common

1) For the last few decades, we've been able to deal with <u>bacterial infections</u> pretty easily using <u>antibiotics</u>. The <u>death rate</u> from infectious bacterial diseases (e.g. pneumonia) has <u>fallen</u> dramatically.

2) But the problem of <u>antibiotic resistance</u> is getting <u>worse</u> — partly because of the <u>overuse</u> and <u>inappropriate use</u> of antibiotics, which has <u>increased</u> the <u>likelihood</u> of people being infected by <u>antibiotic-resistant</u> strains.

3) So antibiotic resistance is a <u>big problem</u> and it's encouraged drug companies to work on developing <u>new</u> antibiotics that are <u>effective</u> against these resistant strains.

4) Meanwhile, bacteria that are resistant to most known antibiotics ('<u>superbugs</u>') are becoming <u>more common</u>.

## Aaargh, a giant earwig! Run from the attack of the superbug...

The reality of <u>superbugs</u> is possibly even scarier than giant earwigs. Actually, nothing's more scary than giant earwigs, but microorganisms that are <u>resistant</u> to <u>all</u> our drugs are a worrying thought. It'll be like going <u>back in time</u> to before antibiotics were invented. So far <u>new drugs</u> have kept us one step ahead, but some people think it's only a matter of time until the options run out.

*\*That's my excuse, you'll have to think of your own.*

# Investigating Antibiotic Action

And now for some hands-on stuff. You can grow your own microorganisms and test how effective different antibiotics or disinfectants are at killing them — just watch out for those bacterial rights activists...

## You can Investigate Antibiotics by Growing Bacteria in the Lab

You can test the action of antibiotics (or disinfectants) by growing cultures of bacteria:

1) Bacteria (and some other microorganisms) are grown (cultured) in a "culture medium". This is usually agar jelly containing the carbohydrates, minerals, proteins and vitamins they need to grow.

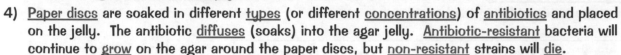

2) Hot agar jelly is poured into shallow round plastic dishes called Petri dishes.

3) When the jelly's cooled and set, inoculating loops (wire loops) are used to transfer microorganisms to the culture medium. The microorganisms then multiply.

4) Paper discs are soaked in different types (or different concentrations) of antibiotics and placed on the jelly. The antibiotic diffuses (soaks) into the agar jelly. Antibiotic-resistant bacteria will continue to grow on the agar around the paper discs, but non-resistant strains will die.

5) To make sure that the results are reliable, a control should be used. This is a paper disc that has not been soaked in an antibiotic. You can then be sure that any difference between the growth of the bacteria around the control disc and around one of the antibiotic discs is due to the effect of the antibiotic alone (and not something weird in the paper, for example).

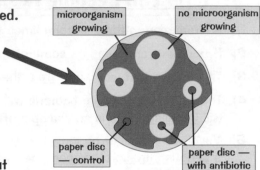

6) The more effective the antibiotic is against the bacteria, the larger the clear area around the paper disc will be.

7) In the lab at school, cultures of microorganisms are kept at about 25 °C because harmful pathogens aren't likely to grow at this temperature.

8) In industrial conditions, cultures are incubated at higher temperatures so that they can grow a lot faster.

## You Need to Make Sure the Experiment Doesn't Get Contaminated

Contamination by unwanted microorganisms will affect your results. To avoid this:

1) The Petri dishes and culture medium must be sterilised before use.

2) The inoculating loop used to transfer the bacteria to the culture medium should be sterilised by passing it through a flame.

3) The Petri dish should have a lid that is kept on before the bacteria are transferred to the culture medium.

4) While transferring the bacteria, the lid of the Petri dish should only be lifted a little bit — to decrease the risk of unwanted microorganisms entering the dish.

5) After transferring the bacteria, the lid of the Petri dish should be lightly taped on — to stop microorganisms from the air getting in.

6) The Petri dish should be stored upside down — to stop bacteria falling onto the agar surface.

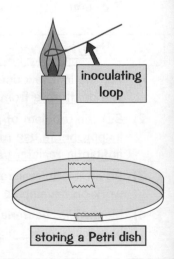

## Agar — my favourite jelly flavour after raspberry...

Microorganisms might be the perfect pets. You don't have to walk them, they won't get lonely and they hardly cost anything to feed. But whatever you do, do not feed them after midnight.

# Revision Summary for Section Five

Well you've fought off that section, but how resistant is it to being remembered?  Time to find out — have a go at these questions.  There'll be an epidemic of questions in the exam, so best vaccinate yourself with some practice now.  OK, I've pushed this whole analogy about as far as it can go now, so I'll shut up...  (But if you find you need a booster, go back through the section to brush up then try this page again.)

1) What is a pathogen?

2) Name two types of pathogen, and describe how each one makes you feel ill.

3) Describe three ways in which your white blood cells defend the body against disease.

4) What are antigens?

5) What are vaccines made of?

6) Which diseases does the MMR vaccine protect you from?

7) Describe how the MMR vaccine works.

8) Give two advantages and two disadvantages of vaccination.

9) What are antibiotics?  Name one.

10) What type of pathogen do antibiotics kill?

11) Why shouldn't your doctor give you antibiotics for the flu?

12) How do bacteria develop resistance to antibiotics?

13) Name one type of bacteria that has developed resistance to antibiotics.

14) Describe an experiment to test the resistance of a microorganism to some different antibiotics.

15) Give three ways in which you would make sure the experiment had not been contaminated by unwanted microorganisms.

# Photosynthesis

First, a <u>photosynthesis equation</u>. You <u>must learn</u> the photosynthesis equation. Learn it so well that you'll <u>still</u> remember it when you're <u>109</u>. Then, at the bottom of this page is a lovely <u>leaf pic</u>. Aaaah.

## Learn the Equations for Photosynthesis:

You can write the equation in <u>words</u> or in <u>chemical symbols</u>. You need to learn <u>both</u>:

$$\text{carbon dioxide} + \text{water} \xrightarrow{\text{LIGHT ENERGY}} \text{glucose} + \text{oxygen}$$

$$6CO_2 + 6H_2O \xrightarrow{\text{LIGHT ENERGY}} C_6H_{12}O_6 + 6O_2$$

## Photosynthesis Produces Glucose Using Sunlight

1) <u>Photosynthesis</u> is the process that produces '<u>food</u>' in plants and algae. The 'food' it produces is <u>glucose</u>.

2) Photosynthesis happens inside the <u>chloroplasts</u>, which are found in <u>some plant cells</u> and in <u>algae</u>.

3) Chloroplasts contain a green substance called <u>chlorophyll</u>.

4) During photosynthesis chlorophyll absorbs <u>light energy</u> from <u>sunlight</u> and uses it to convert <u>carbon dioxide</u> (from the air) and <u>water</u> (from the soil) into <u>glucose</u>.

5) <u>Oxygen</u> is also produced as a by-product.

6) Photosynthesis happens in the <u>leaves</u> of all <u>green plants</u> — this is largely what the leaves are for.

Below is a cross-section of a leaf showing the <u>four</u> raw materials needed for <u>photosynthesis</u>.

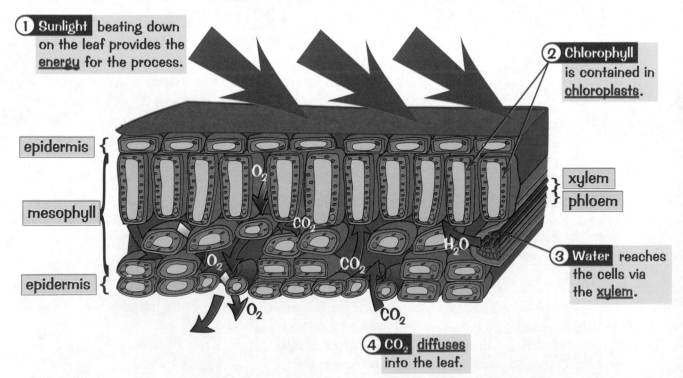

① Sunlight beating down on the leaf provides the energy for the process.

② Chlorophyll is contained in chloroplasts.

③ Water reaches the cells via the xylem.

④ CO₂ diffuses into the leaf.

epidermis

mesophyll

epidermis

xylem

phloem

## Now you'll have something to bore the great-grandkids with...

You'll be able to tell them how in your day, all you needed was a bit of carbon dioxide and some water and you could make your own entertainment. See, when you're 109 you're allowed to get a bit confused, but in the middle of an exam you most certainly are not. So if you don't know it, <u>learn it</u>. (And if you do, learn it again anyway.)

# The Rate of Photosynthesis

The rate of photosynthesis is affected by the intensity of <u>light</u>, the volume of <u>$CO_2$</u>, and the <u>temperature</u>. Plants also need <u>water</u> for photosynthesis, but when a plant is so short of water that it becomes the <u>limiting factor</u> in photosynthesis, it's already in such <u>trouble</u> that this is the least of its worries.

## The Limiting Factor Depends on the Conditions

1) These three factors (<u>light</u>, <u>$CO_2$</u> and <u>temperature</u>) <u>interact</u> and <u>any one</u> of them can become the <u>limiting factor</u> (which just means that it's stopping photosynthesis from happening any <u>faster</u>).

2) Which factor is limiting at a particular time depends on the <u>environmental conditions</u>:

   • at <u>night</u> it's pretty obvious that <u>light</u> is the limiting factor (also when it's <u>gloomy</u>, e.g. <u>dusk</u> or <u>dawn</u>)

   • in <u>winter</u> it's often the <u>temperature</u>

   • if it's warm enough and bright enough, the amount of <u>$CO_2$</u> is usually limiting.

You can do <u>experiments</u> to work out the <u>ideal conditions</u> for photosynthesis in a particular plant. The easiest type to use is a water plant like <u>Canadian pondweed</u> — you can easily measure the amount of <u>oxygen produced</u> in a given time to show how <u>fast</u> photosynthesis is happening (remember, oxygen is made during photosynthesis).

You could either count the <u>bubbles</u> given off, or if you want to be a bit more <u>accurate</u> you could <u>collect</u> the oxygen in a <u>gas syringe</u>.

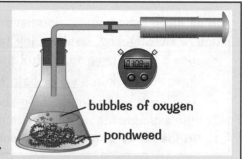

bubbles of oxygen

pondweed

## Three Important Graphs for Rate of Photosynthesis

### 1) Not Enough Light Slows Down the Rate of Photosynthesis

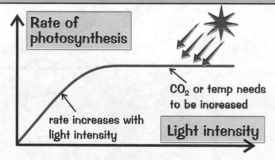

Rate of photosynthesis

rate increases with light intensity

$CO_2$ or temp needs to be increased

Light intensity

1) Light provides the <u>energy</u> needed for photosynthesis.

2) As the <u>light level</u> is raised, the rate of photosynthesis <u>increases steadily</u> — but only up to a <u>certain point</u>.

3) Beyond that, it <u>won't</u> make any difference because then it'll be either the <u>temperature</u> or the <u>$CO_2$ level</u> which is the limiting factor.

4) In the lab you can change the light intensity by <u>moving a lamp</u> closer to or further away from your plant.

5) But if you just plot the rate of photosynthesis against "distance of lamp from the beaker", you get a <u>weird-shaped graph</u>. To get a graph like the one above you either need to <u>measure</u> the light intensity at the beaker using a <u>light meter</u> or do a bit of nifty maths with your results.

### 2) Too Little Carbon Dioxide Also Slows it Down

1) $CO_2$ is one of the <u>raw materials</u> needed for photosynthesis.

2) As with light intensity the amount of <u>$CO_2$</u> will only increase the rate of photosynthesis up to a point. After this the graph <u>flattens out</u> showing that $CO_2$ is no longer the <u>limiting factor</u>.

3) As long as <u>light</u> and <u>$CO_2$</u> are in plentiful supply then the factor limiting photosynthesis must be <u>temperature</u>.

4) There are loads of different ways to control the amount of $CO_2$. One way is to dissolve different amounts of <u>sodium hydrogencarbonate</u> in the water, which <u>gives off</u> $CO_2$.

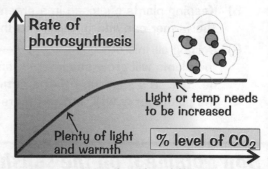

Rate of photosynthesis

Light or temp needs to be increased

Plenty of light and warmth

% level of $CO_2$

# The Rate of Photosynthesis

## 3) The Temperature has to be Just Right

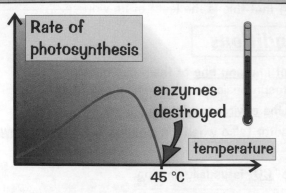

Rate of photosynthesis

enzymes destroyed

temperature

45 °C

1) Usually, if the temperature is the <u>limiting factor</u> it's because it's <u>too low</u> — the <u>enzymes</u> needed for photosynthesis work more <u>slowly</u> at low temperatures.

2) But if the plant gets <u>too hot</u>, the enzymes it needs for photosynthesis and its other reactions will be <u>damaged</u>.

3) This happens at about <u>45 °C</u> (which is pretty hot for outdoors, although <u>greenhouses</u> can get that hot if you're not careful).

4) Experimentally, the best way to control the temperature of the flask is to put it in a <u>water bath</u>.

In all these experiments, you have to try and keep all the variables <u>constant</u> apart from the one you're investigating, so it's a <u>fair test</u>:

- use a <u>bench lamp</u> to control the intensity of the light (careful not to <u>block the light</u> with anything)
- keep the flask in a <u>water bath</u> to help keep the temperature constant
- you <u>can't</u> really do anything about the $CO_2$ levels — you just have to use a <u>large flask</u>, and do the experiments as <u>quickly</u> as you can, so that the plant doesn't use up too much of the $CO_2$ in the flask. If you're using sodium hydrogencarbonate make sure it's changed each time.

## You can Artificially Create the Ideal Conditions for Farming

1) The most common way to artificially create the <u>ideal environment</u> for plants is to grow them in a <u>greenhouse</u>.

2) Greenhouses help to <u>trap</u> the sun's <u>heat</u>, and make sure that the <u>temperature</u> doesn't become <u>limiting</u>. In winter a farmer or gardener might use a <u>heater</u> as well to keep the temperature at the ideal level. In summer it could get <u>too hot</u>, so they might use <u>shades</u> and <u>ventilation</u> to cool things down.

3) <u>Light</u> is always needed for photosynthesis, so commercial farmers often supply <u>artificial light</u> after the sun goes down to give their plants more quality photosynthesis time.

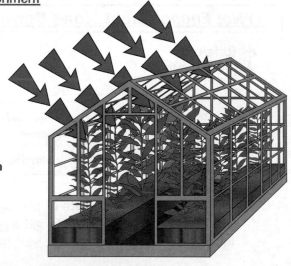

4) Farmers and gardeners can also increase the level of <u>carbon dioxide</u> in the greenhouse. A fairly common way is to use a <u>paraffin heater</u> to heat the greenhouse. As the paraffin burns, it makes carbon dioxide as a <u>by-product</u>.

5) Keeping plants <u>enclosed</u> in a greenhouse also makes it easier to keep them free from <u>pests</u> and <u>diseases</u>. The farmer can add <u>fertilisers</u> to the soil as well, to provide all the <u>minerals</u> needed for healthy growth.

6) Sorting all this out <u>costs money</u> — but if the farmer can keep the conditions <u>just right</u> for photosynthesis, the plants will grow much <u>faster</u> and a <u>decent crop</u> can be harvested much more <u>often</u>, which can then be <u>sold</u>. It's important that a farmer supplies just the <u>right amount</u> of heat, light, etc. — enough to make the plants grow well, but <u>not</u> more than the plants <u>need</u>, as this would just be <u>wasting money</u>.

## Don't blame it on the sunshine, don't blame it on the $CO_2$...

...don't blame it on the temperature, blame it on the plant. Right, and now you'll never forget the three limiting factors in photosynthesis. No... well, make sure you read these pages over and over again till you do. With your newly found knowledge of photosynthesis you could take over the world...

# How Plants Use Glucose

Once plants have <u>made glucose</u> by photosynthesis (see page 58), there are a <u>few ways</u> they can <u>use</u> it.

## ① For Respiration

1) Plants manufacture <u>glucose</u> in their <u>leaves</u>.

2) They then use some of the glucose for <u>respiration</u> (see page 29).

3) This <u>releases energy</u> which enables them to <u>convert</u> the rest of the glucose into various <u>other useful substances</u>, which they can use to <u>build new cells</u> and <u>grow</u>.

4) To produce some of these substances they also need to <u>gather</u> a few <u>minerals</u> from the soil.

## ② Making Cell Walls

<u>Glucose</u> is converted into <u>cellulose</u> for making strong <u>cell walls</u> (see page 12), especially in a rapidly growing plant.

*Algae also use glucose to make cellulose for cell walls, fats and oils for storage, and amino acids for proteins.*

## ③ Making Proteins

<u>Glucose</u> is combined with <u>nitrate ions</u> (absorbed from the soil) to make <u>amino acids</u>, which are then made into <u>proteins</u>.

<u>Carnivorous</u> plants like the <u>Venus Fly Trap</u> are <u>adapted</u> to live in <u>nutrient poor soil</u> — they get most of the nutrients they need (e.g. nitrates) from the <u>animals</u> (e.g. insects) that they <u>catch</u>. (Yum).

## ④ Stored as Fats or Oils

<u>Glucose</u> is turned into <u>lipids</u> (fats and oils) for storing in <u>seeds</u>. <u>Sunflower seeds</u>, for example, contain a lot of oil — we get <u>cooking oil</u> and <u>margarine</u> from them. Seeds also store <u>starch</u> (see below).

## ⑤ Stored as Starch

<u>Glucose</u> is turned into <u>starch</u> and <u>stored</u> in roots, stems and leaves, ready for use when photosynthesis isn't happening, like in the <u>winter</u>.

<u>Starch</u> is <u>insoluble</u> which makes it much <u>better</u> for <u>storing</u> than glucose — a cell with <u>lots of glucose</u> in would draw in loads of water and <u>swell up</u>.

<u>Potato</u> and <u>parsnip</u> plants store a lot of starch underground over the winter so a <u>new plant</u> can grow from it the following spring. We eat the swollen storage organs.

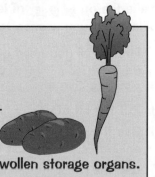

## For making small ornamental birdcages...

Actually, I made that last one up. I was bored. So there are actually only five things to learn that plants do with glucose. Right, shut the book right now. Or actually, finish reading this and then shut the book. Then write down all five uses of glucose from memory. Bet you forget one. <u>Repeat until you don't</u>.

# Exchanging Materials in Plants

Plants are fussy and shop around for the things they need to <u>stay alive</u> — carbon dioxide from the <u>air</u>, water and minerals from the soil. But they need to <u>move</u> everything to the place in the plant where it's <u>used</u>...

## Leaves and Roots Help Plants Exchange Materials with the Air and Soil

In flowering plants:

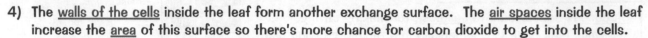
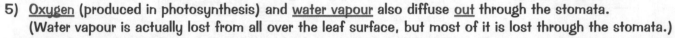
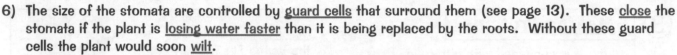

1) Carbon dioxide <u>diffuses into the air spaces</u> within the leaf, then it <u>diffuses into the cells</u> where photosynthesis happens. The leaf's structure is <u>adapted</u> so that this happens easily.

2) The underneath of the leaf is an <u>exchange surface</u>. It's covered in biddy little holes called <u>stomata</u> which the carbon dioxide diffuses in through.

Oxygen and water vapour diffuse out of the leaf

$CO_2$ diffuses into leaf

Hot dry wind
good for carrying the water vapour away

3) The <u>flattened shape</u> of the leaf increases the <u>area</u> of the exchange surface so that it's more effective.

4) The <u>walls of the cells</u> inside the leaf form another exchange surface. The <u>air spaces</u> inside the leaf increase the <u>area</u> of this surface so there's more chance for carbon dioxide to get into the cells.

5) <u>Oxygen</u> (produced in photosynthesis) and <u>water vapour</u> also diffuse <u>out</u> through the stomata. (Water vapour is actually lost from all over the leaf surface, but most of it is lost through the stomata.)

6) The size of the stomata are controlled by <u>guard cells</u> that surround them (see page 13). These <u>close</u> the stomata if the plant is <u>losing water faster</u> than it is being replaced by the roots. Without these guard cells the plant would soon <u>wilt</u>.

> The water vapour <u>evaporates</u> from the cells inside the leaf. Then it escapes by <u>diffusion</u> because there's a lot of it <u>inside</u> the leaf and less of it in the <u>air outside</u>. Evaporation is <u>quickest</u> in <u>hot</u>, <u>dry</u>, <u>windy conditions</u> — and don't you forget it!

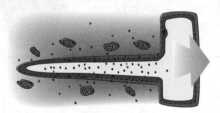

7) Most of the <u>water</u> and <u>mineral ions</u> needed by the plant are absorbed by the <u>roots</u>.

8) The <u>surface area</u> of roots is increased by <u>root hairs</u> — so stuff can be absorbed much more <u>quickly</u> (see p. 19).

## You can Look at Leaf Cells under a Microscope

You can't see through a <u>whole leaf</u> — it's too <u>thick</u>. But you can see through the <u>epidermis</u>. This is the <u>outer layer</u> of leaf cells (see page 15) and it's <u>transparent</u>. Here's how you'd <u>mount</u> a bit of epidermis if you wanted to look at it under a microscope:

1) First of all you need your <u>bit of epidermis</u>, a <u>slide</u>, a <u>coverslip</u>, a <u>pipette</u> with some <u>water</u> in it and a <u>mounted needle</u>.

2) Put the bit of <u>epidermis</u> in the <u>centre</u> of your <u>slide</u>.

3) Use the <u>pipette</u> to put a <u>drop of water</u> on the epidermis — this just helps to keep it in place.

4) Use the <u>mounted needle</u> to carefully <u>lower</u> the <u>coverslip</u> onto the drop of water.

5) Bung it on your 'scope and Bob's your uncle — you have a <u>lovely leaf</u> to look at. Lucky you.

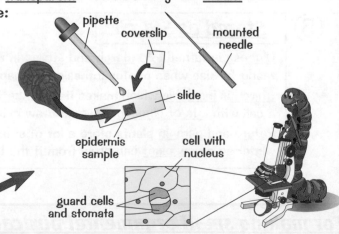

pipette
coverslip
mounted needle
slide
epidermis sample
cell with nucleus
guard cells and stomata

## I say stomaaaarta, you say stomaaaayta...

Leaves are a bit like <u>washing</u> that's been hung outside — they dry out much faster on a <u>hot</u>, <u>dry</u>, <u>windy</u> day.

# Water Flow Through Plants

Flowering plants have <u>two</u> separate types of vessel — <u>xylem</u> and <u>phloem</u> — for transporting stuff around. <u>Both</u> types of vessel go to <u>every part</u> of the plant, but they are totally <u>separate</u>.

Food (mainly dissolved sugars)

### Phloem Tubes Transport Food:

1) Made of columns of living cells with small <u>holes</u> <u>in the ends</u> to allow stuff to flow through.

2) They transport <u>food substances</u> (mainly dissolved <u>sugars</u>) made in the leaves to <u>growing regions</u> (e.g. new shoots) and <u>storage organs</u> (e.g. root tubers) of the plant.

3) The transport goes in <u>both directions</u>.

4) This process is called <u>translocation</u>.

### Xylem Tubes Take Water UP:

1) Made of <u>dead cells</u> joined end to end with <u>no</u> end walls between them and a hole down the middle.

2) They carry <u>water</u> and <u>minerals</u> from the <u>roots</u> to the <u>stem</u> and <u>leaves</u>.

3) The movement of water <u>from</u> the <u>roots</u>, <u>through</u> the <u>xylem</u> and <u>out</u> of the <u>leaves</u> is called the <u>transpiration stream</u> (see below).

Water and minerals

## Transpiration is the Loss of Water from the Plant

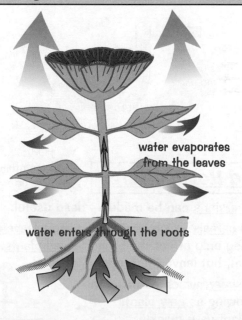

water evaporates from the leaves

water enters through the roots

1) Transpiration is caused by the <u>evaporation</u> and <u>diffusion</u> (see page 62) of water from inside the leaves.

2) This creates a slight <u>shortage</u> of water in the leaf, and so more water is drawn up from the rest of the plant through the <u>xylem vessels</u> to replace it.

3) This in turn means more water is drawn up from the <u>roots</u>, and so there's a constant <u>transpiration stream</u> of water through the plant.

4) Transpiration is just a <u>side-effect</u> of the way leaves are adapted for <u>photosynthesis</u>. They have to have <u>stomata</u> in them so that gases can be exchanged easily. Because there's more water <u>inside</u> the plant than in the <u>air outside</u>, the water escapes from the leaves through the stomata.

## *Transpiration — the plant version of perspiration...*

Here's an interesting fact (well, sort of...) — a biggish tree loses about a <u>thousand litres</u> of water from its leaves <u>every single day</u>. That's as much water as the average person drinks in a whole year, so the <u>roots</u> have to be very effective at drawing in water from the soil. Which is why they have all those root <u>hairs</u>, you see.

# Plant Hormones

Plants might not have mood swings in the same way people do, but they do have <u>hormones</u>. Hormones make sure plants grow in a <u>useful direction</u> (e.g. towards light).

## Auxin is a Plant Growth Hormone

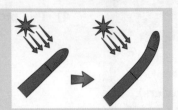

1) <u>Auxin</u> is a <u>plant hormone</u> that controls <u>growth</u> near the <u>tips</u> of <u>shoots</u> and <u>roots</u>.

2) It controls the growth of a plant in response to <u>light</u> (<u>phototropism</u>), <u>gravity</u> (<u>gravitropism</u> or <u>geotropism</u>) and <u>moisture</u> (<u>hydrotropism</u>).

3) Auxin is produced in the <u>tips</u> and <u>moves backwards</u> to stimulate the <u>cell elongation</u> (<u>enlargement</u>) <u>process</u> which occurs in the cells <u>just behind</u> the tips.

4) If the tip of a shoot is <u>removed</u>, no auxin is available and the shoot may <u>stop growing</u>.

5) Extra auxin <u>promotes</u> growth in the <u>shoot</u> but <u>inhibits</u> growth in the <u>root</u> — producing the <u>desired result</u>...

### Shoots grow towards light

1) When a <u>shoot tip</u> is exposed to <u>light</u>, <u>more auxin</u> accumulates on the side that's in the <u>shade</u> than the side that's in the light.

2) This makes the cells grow (elongate) <u>faster</u> on the <u>shaded side</u>, so the shoot bends <u>towards</u> the light.

### Shoots grow away from gravity

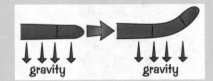

1) When a <u>shoot</u> is growing sideways, <u>gravity</u> produces an unequal distribution of auxin in the tip, with <u>more auxin</u> on the <u>lower side</u>.

2) This causes the lower side to grow <u>faster</u>, bending the shoot <u>upwards</u>.

### Roots grow towards gravity

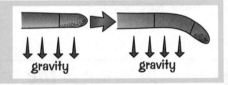

1) A <u>root</u> growing sideways will also have more auxin on its <u>lower side</u>.

2) But in a root the <u>extra</u> auxin <u>inhibits</u> growth. This means the cells on <u>top</u> elongate faster, and the root bends <u>downwards</u>.

### Roots grow towards moisture

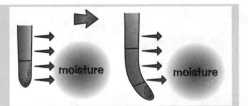

1) An uneven amount of moisture either side of a root produces <u>more auxin</u> on the side with <u>more moisture</u>.

2) This <u>inhibits</u> growth on that side, causing the root to bend in that direction, <u>towards the moisture</u>.

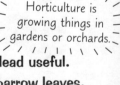
Horticulture is growing things in gardens or orchards.

## Plant Hormones have Uses in Agriculture and Horticulture

Plant hormones can be <u>extracted</u> and used by people, or <u>artificial versions</u> can be made — dead useful.

1) Most <u>weeds</u> in crop fields are <u>broad-leaved</u>, unlike <u>grasses</u> and <u>cereals</u> which have very <u>narrow leaves</u>. <u>Selective weedkillers</u> are made of <u>plant growth hormones</u> — they only affect the <u>broad-leaved plants</u>. They <u>disrupt</u> their normal growth patterns, which soon <u>kills</u> them, but leave the crops <u>untouched</u>.

2) Plant cuttings <u>won't always grow</u> in soil. If you add <u>rooting powder</u>, which contains the plant hormone <u>auxin</u>, they'll <u>produce roots</u> rapidly and start growing as <u>new plants</u>. This helps growers to produce lots of <u>clones</u> of a really good plant <u>very quickly</u>.

boring old soil
rooting compound

## A plant auxin to a bar — 'ouch'...

Learn the page. Learn the <u>whole darn page</u>. There's no getting out of it folks.

# Sexual Reproduction in Plants

Some people think <u>flowers</u> are a bit girly. Well they may be in touch with their feminine side, but they actually have both <u>female</u> and <u>male</u> parts. Clever, huh.

## The Flower Contains both Male and Female Structures

For a flowering plant to reproduce <u>sexually</u>, it needs to:

1) Produce <u>male</u> and <u>female</u> gametes.
2) <u>Transfer</u> the male <u>gametes</u> to female <u>ovules</u> (where the female <u>gametes</u> are) — this is called <u>pollination</u>.
3) Undergo <u>fertilisation</u> — this is when the <u>gametes fuse together</u> (see below).
   After fertilisation the ovules <u>grow</u> into <u>seeds</u> inside a <u>fruit</u>.

<u>Pollen</u> can also be transferred from the <u>anther</u> of <u>one plant</u> to the <u>stigma</u> of a <u>different plant</u>. This is called <u>cross pollination</u>.

You might have to <u>label</u> a flower's <u>reproductive system</u> in the exam — so here's what one looks like:

### The Stamen is the Male Reproductive Part

The <u>stamen</u> consists of the <u>anther</u> and <u>filament</u>:

The ANTHER contains <u>pollen grains</u> — these produce the <u>male gametes</u> (sperm).

The FILAMENT is the <u>stalk</u> that <u>supports</u> the anther.

### The Carpel is the Female Reproductive Part

The <u>carpel</u> consists of the <u>stigma</u>, <u>style</u> and <u>ovary</u>

The STIGMA is the <u>end</u> bit that the <u>pollen</u> grains <u>attach</u> to.

The STYLE is the rod-like section that <u>supports</u> the stigma.

The OVARY contains the <u>female gametes</u> (eggs) inside <u>ovules</u>.

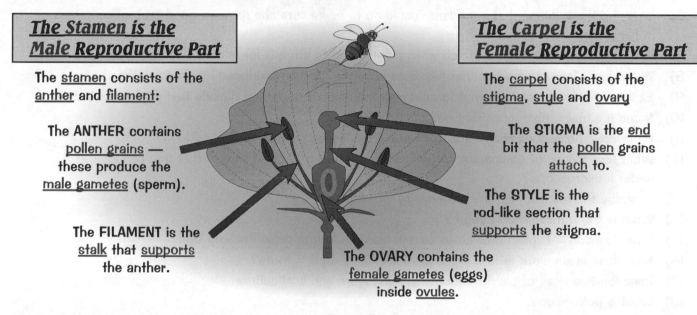

## Fertilisation Produces Seeds Containing Plant Embryos

It's quite complicated but this is <u>everything</u> you need to know about what goes on during <u>sexual reproduction</u>.

1) The <u>anther</u> produces the <u>male gametes</u> in <u>pollen grains</u>.
2) A <u>pollen</u> grain lands on the <u>stigma</u> — the top of the female <u>carpel</u>.
3) A <u>pollen tube</u> grows out of the pollen grain, down through the <u>style</u> to the <u>ovary</u> and into the <u>ovule</u> (where the female gametes are).
4) A <u>nucleus</u> from a male gamete then <u>moves down the tube</u> into the <u>ovary</u> where it <u>fertilises</u> the <u>egg cell nucleus</u> in the ovule. Fertilisation is when the two nuclei <u>fuse</u> together to make a <u>zygote</u>. The zygote divides by <u>mitosis</u> to form an <u>embryo</u> (for more on mitosis see page 23).
5) At the same time <u>other nuclei</u> from the male gametes fertilise <u>endosperm nuclei</u> in the ovule. This produces the <u>endosperm</u> — a '<u>food sac</u>' that stores starch to feed the growing embryo.
6) The endosperm <u>plus</u> the female tissues of the ovule make up a <u>seed</u>. The <u>ovary</u> develops into a <u>fruit</u> around the seed.

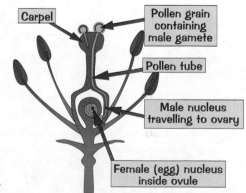

## There's no stigma attached to it...

It's a bit weird to think of plants reproducing <u>sexually</u> — it just means that the <u>male gametes</u> (in the pollen) fertilise the <u>female gametes</u> (in the ovary). Not quite so weird after all... hmmm.

# Revision Summary for Section Six

And where do you think you're going? It's no use just reading through and thinking you've got it all — this stuff will only stick in your head if you've learnt it <u>properly</u>. And that's what these questions are for. I won't pretend they'll be easy — they're not meant to be, but all the information's in the section somewhere. Have a go at all the questions, then if there are any you can't answer, go back, look stuff up and try again. Enjoy...

1) Write down the equation for photosynthesis in: a) words   b) chemical symbols.
2) What is the green substance in leaves that absorbs light energy?
3) Name the three factors that can limit the rate of photosynthesis.
4) You carry out an experiment where you change the light intensity experienced by a piece of Canadian pondweed by changing the distance between the pondweed and a lamp supplying it with light. Write down three important things which must be kept constant for this experiment to be a fair test.
5) Explain why it's important that a plant doesn't get too hot.
6) Describe three things that a gardener could do to make sure she grows a good crop of tomatoes in her greenhouse.
7) Why is glucose turned into starch when plants need to store it for later?
8) Write down four other ways that plants can use the glucose produced by photosynthesis.
9) Explain how leaves are adapted to maximise the amount of carbon dioxide that gets to their cells.
10) Name the main substances that diffuse out of leaves.
11) What conditions does evaporation of water from leaves happen most quickly in?
12) What four pieces of equipment do you need to mount a piece of leaf so that you can look at it under a microscope?
13) Describe the role of: a) the phloem   b) the xylem.
14) What is the transpiration stream?
15) What is auxin? Explain how auxin causes plant shoots to grow towards light.
16) How does auxin work differently in plant shoots and plant roots?
17) Describe two uses of plant hormones in agriculture and horticulture.
18) What is pollination?
19) Which part of the flower produces the male gametes?
20) Where are the female gametes located in the flower?
21) Describe the stages of sexual reproduction in flowering plants.

(That last one was a biggie so I'll stop now).

# Variation

You'll probably have noticed that not all people are identical.  There are reasons for this.

## Organisms of the Same Species Have Differences

1) Different species look... well... different — my dog definitely doesn't look like a daisy.

2) But even organisms of the <u>same species</u> will usually look at least <u>slightly</u> different — e.g. in a room full of people you'll see different <u>colour hair</u>, individually <u>shaped noses</u>, a variety of <u>heights</u> etc.

3) These differences are called the <u>variation</u> within a species — and there are <u>two</u> types of variation:  <u>genetic variation</u> and <u>environmental variation</u>.

## Different Genes Cause Genetic Variation

1) All plants and animals have <u>characteristics</u> that are in some ways similar to their <u>parents'</u> (e.g. I've got my dad's nose, apparently).

2) This is because an organism's <u>characteristics</u> are determined by the <u>genes inherited</u> from their <u>parents</u>. (Genes are the <u>codes</u> inside your cells that <u>control</u> how you're made — more about these on page 68).

3) These genes are passed on in <u>sex cells</u> (<u>gametes</u>), which the offspring develop from (see page 24).

4) Most animals (and quite a lot of plants) get <u>some</u> genes from the <u>mother</u> and <u>some</u> from the <u>father</u>.

5) This combining of genes from two parents causes <u>genetic variation</u> — no two of the species are <u>genetically identical</u> (other than identical twins).

6) <u>Some</u> characteristics are determined <u>only</u> by genes (e.g. violet flower colour).  In <u>animals</u> these include: <u>eye colour</u>, <u>blood group</u> and <u>inherited disorders</u> (e.g. haemophilia or cystic fibrosis).

## Characteristics are also Influenced by the Environment

1) The <u>environment</u> that organisms <u>live and grow</u> in also causes <u>differences</u> between members of the same species — this is called <u>environmental variation</u>.

2) Environmental variation covers a <u>wide range</u> of differences — from <u>losing your toes</u> in a piranha attack, to getting a <u>suntan</u>, to having <u>yellow leaves</u> (never happened to me yet though), and so on.

A plant grown on a nice sunny windowsill would grow <u>luscious</u> and <u>green</u>.

The same plant grown in darkness would grow <u>tall and spindly</u> and its leaves would turn <u>yellow</u> — these are <u>environmental variations</u>.

3) Basically, <u>any difference</u> that has been caused by the <u>conditions</u> something lives in, is an <u>environmental variation</u>.

## Most Characteristics are Due to Genes AND the Environment

1) <u>Most characteristics</u> (e.g. body weight, height, skin colour, condition of teeth, academic or athletic prowess, etc.) are determined by a <u>mixture</u> of <u>genetic</u> and <u>environmental</u> factors.

2) For example, the <u>maximum height</u> that an animal or plant could grow to is determined by its <u>genes</u>. But whether it actually grows that tall depends on its <u>environment</u> (e.g. how much food it gets).

## My mum's got no trousers — cos I've got her jeans...

So, you are the way you are partly because of the genes you inherited off your folks.  But you can't blame it <u>all</u> on your parents, since your <u>environment</u> then takes over and begins to mould you in all sorts of ways. In fact, it's often really tricky to decide which factor is <u>more influential</u>, your genes or the environment — a good way to study this is with <u>identical twins</u>.

# The Structure of DNA

The first step in understanding genetics is getting to grips with <u>DNA</u>.

## Chromosomes Are Really Long Molecules of DNA

1) <u>DNA</u> stands for <u>deoxyribonucleic acid</u>.

2) DNA contains <u>coded information</u> — basically all the <u>instructions</u> to put an organism together and <u>make it work</u>.

3) So it's <u>what's in your DNA</u> that determines <u>what inherited characteristics</u> you have.

4) DNA is found in the <u>nucleus</u> of animal and plant cells, in really <u>long molecules</u> called <u>chromosomes</u>.

5) <u>Chromosomes</u> normally come in <u>pairs</u>.

*Some of this might seem familiar from page 22.*

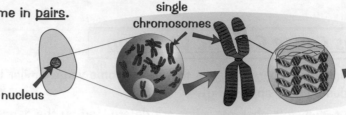

single chromosomes

nucleus

A DNA molecule with a double helix structure — see below

## A Gene Codes for a Specific Protein

1) A <u>gene</u> is a <u>section</u> of DNA.

2) Each gene <u>codes for</u> (tells the cells to make) a <u>particular combination</u> of <u>amino acids</u> which are put together to make a <u>specific protein</u>.

3) Only <u>20</u> amino acids are used, but they make up <u>thousands</u> of different <u>proteins</u>.

4) Genes simply tell cells <u>in what order</u> to put the amino acids together (more on this below).

5) DNA also determines what <u>proteins</u> the cell <u>produces</u>, e.g. haemoglobin, keratin.

6) That in turn determines what <u>type of cell</u> it is, e.g. red blood cell, skin cell.

## DNA is a Double Helix

1) A DNA molecule has <u>two long strands</u> coiled together in the shape of a <u>double helix</u> (a double-stranded spiral).

2) The two strands are held together by chemicals called <u>bases</u>.

3) There are <u>four</u> different bases (shown in our diagrams as different colours) — (A), (T), (C), and (G).

4) It's the <u>order</u> of <u>bases</u> in a <u>gene</u> that decides the order of <u>amino acids</u> in a <u>protein</u>.

5) Each amino acid is <u>coded for</u> by a sequence of <u>three bases</u> in the gene.

6) The amino acids are <u>joined together</u> to make proteins, following the order of the bases in the gene.

strands

bases

base on one strand is joined to a base on the other by cross links

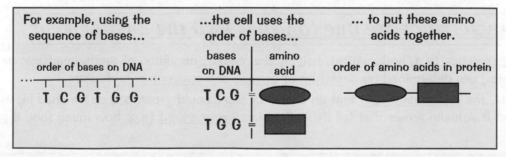

| For example, using the sequence of bases... | ...the cell uses the order of bases... | | ... to put these amino acids together. |
|---|---|---|---|
| order of bases on DNA | bases on DNA | amino acid | order of amino acids in protein |
| T C G T G G | T C G | | |
| | T G G | | |

## Q: What do DNA and a game of rounders have in common...?

**A:** <u>four bases</u>. A little light relief for you there. But let's not get distracted. Genes are important because they control what <u>characteristics</u> you have (passed on from your parents). <u>Genes</u> control the <u>proteins</u> that are made, and <u>proteins</u> control most processes in the body (including your characteristics).

# X and Y Chromosomes

Now for a couple of very important little chromosomes...

## Your Chromosomes Control Whether You're Male or Female

There are <u>23 pairs</u> of chromosomes in every human body cell (see page 22).  Of these <u>22</u> are <u>matched pairs</u> of chromosomes.  The <u>23rd pair</u> are labelled <u>XY</u> or <u>XX</u>.  They're the two chromosomes that decide whether you turn out <u>male</u> or <u>female</u>.

> <u>All men</u> have an <u>X</u> and a <u>Y</u> chromosome:   XY
> The <u>Y chromosome</u> causes <u>male characteristics</u>.
>
> <u>All women</u> have <u>two X chromosomes</u>:   XX
> The <u>XX combination</u> allows <u>female characteristics</u> to develop.

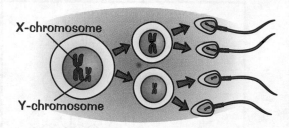

When making sperm, the **X** and **Y** chromosomes are drawn apart in the first division in <u>meiosis</u> (see page 24).  There's a <u>50% chance</u> each sperm cell gets an <u>X-chromosome</u> and a <u>50% chance</u> it gets a <u>Y-chromosome</u>.

A similar thing happens when making eggs.  But the original cell has two X-chromosomes, so all the eggs have one X-chromosome.

## Genetic Diagrams Show the Possible Combinations of Gametes

1) To find the <u>probability</u> of getting a boy or a girl, you can draw a <u>genetic diagram</u>.

2) Genetic diagrams are just <u>models</u> that are used to show all the possible genetic <u>outcomes</u> when you <u>cross together</u> different genes or chromosomes.

3) Put the <u>possible gametes</u> (eggs or sperm) from <u>one</u> parent down the side, and those from the <u>other</u> parent along the top.

4) Then in each middle square you <u>fill in</u> the letters from the top and side that line up with that square.  The <u>pairs of letters</u> in the middle show the possible combinations of the gametes.

5) There are <u>two XX results</u> and <u>two XY results</u>, so there's the same probability of getting a boy or a girl.

6) Don't forget that this <u>50:50 ratio</u> is only a <u>probability</u> at each pregnancy.  If you had four kids they <u>could</u> all be <u>boys</u> — yes I know, terrifying isn't it?

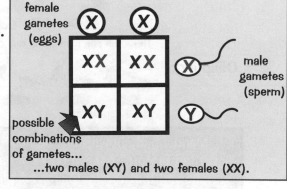

...two males (XY) and two females (XX).

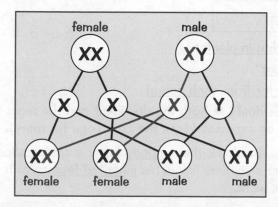

The other type of genetic diagram looks a bit more complicated, but it shows exactly the same thing.

1) At the top are the <u>parents</u>.

2) The middle circles show the <u>possible gametes</u> that are formed.  One gamete from the female combines with one gamete from the male (during fertilisation).

3) The criss-cross lines show <u>all</u> the <u>possible</u> ways the X and Y chromosomes <u>could</u> combine.  The <u>possible combinations</u> of the offspring are shown in the bottom circles.

4) Remember, only <u>one</u> of these possibilities would <u>actually happen</u> for any one offspring.

## Have you got the Y-factor...

Most genetic diagrams you'll see in exams concentrate on a <u>gene</u>, instead of a <u>chromosome</u>. But the principle's the same.  Don't worry — there are loads of other examples on the following pages.

# The Work of Mendel

Some people forget about Mendel but I reckon he's the <u>Granddaddy of Genetics</u>. Here's a whole page on him.

## Mendel Did Genetic Experiments with Pea Plants

<u>Gregor Mendel</u> was an Austrian monk who trained in <u>mathematics</u> and <u>natural history</u> at the University of Vienna. On his garden plot at the monastery, Mendel noted how <u>characteristics</u> in <u>plants</u> were <u>passed on</u> from one generation to the next.

The results of his research were published in <u>1866</u> and eventually became the <u>foundation</u> of modern <u>genetics</u>.

The diagrams show two <u>crosses for height</u> in <u>pea plants</u> that Mendel carried out...

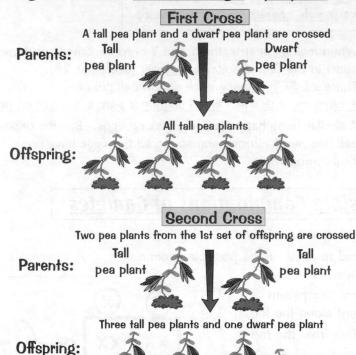

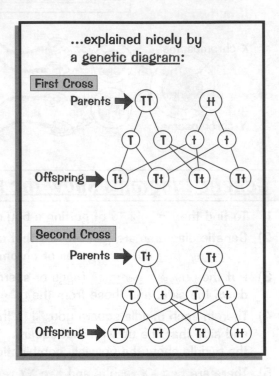

...explained nicely by a <u>genetic diagram</u>:

> Mendel had shown that the height characteristic in pea plants was determined by separate "<u>inherited factors</u>" passed on from each parent. The ratios of tall and dwarf plants in the offspring showed that the factor for tall plants, <u>T</u>, was <u>dominant</u> over the factor for dwarf plants, <u>t</u>.

## Mendel Reached Three Important Conclusions

Mendel reached these three important conclusions about <u>heredity in plants</u>:

1) Characteristics in plants are determined by "<u>inherited factors</u>".

2) Inherited factors are passed on from both parents, <u>one factor</u> from <u>each parent</u>.

3) Inherited factors can be <u>dominant</u> or <u>recessive</u> — if an individual has <u>both</u> the dominant and the recessive factor for a characteristic, the <u>dominant</u> characteristic will be expressed (see the next page for more).

We now know that the "inherited factors" are of course <u>genes</u>. But back then <u>nobody</u> knew anything about DNA. It wasn't until a long time after Mendel's death that other scientists linked his <u>inherited factors</u> with <u>genes</u> and <u>chromosomes</u> — and realised the <u>significance</u> of his work.

## Clearly, being a monk in the 1800s was a right laugh...

Well, there was no TV in those days, you see. Monks had to make their <u>own entertainment</u>. And in Mendel's case, that involved growing lots and lots of <u>peas</u>. He was a very clever lad, was Mendel, but unfortunately just a bit <u>ahead of his time</u>. Nobody had a clue what he was going on about.

# Genetic Diagrams

Genetic diagrams, eh. They're not as scary as they look — you just need to practise them...

## Some Characteristics are Controlled by Single Genes

1) What genes you inherit control what characteristics you develop — genes work at a molecular level to develop the characteristics that can be seen.

2) Different genes control different characteristics.

3) Some characteristics are controlled by a single gene. Others are controlled by lots of genes.

4) All genes exist in different versions called alleles (which are represented by letters in genetic diagrams).

5) You have two versions (alleles) of every gene in your body — one on each chromosome in a pair.

6) If an organism has two alleles for a particular gene that are the same, then it's homozygous. If its two alleles for a particular gene are different, then it's heterozygous.

7) If the two alleles are different, only one can determine what characteristic is present. The allele for the characteristic that's shown is called the dominant allele (use a capital letter for dominant alleles — e.g. 'C'). The other one is called recessive (and you show these with small letters — e.g. 'c').

8) For an organism to display a recessive characteristic, both its alleles must be recessive (e.g. cc). But to display a dominant characteristic the organism can be either CC or Cc, because the dominant allele overrules the recessive one if the plant/animal/other organism is heterozygous.

9) Your genotype is which alleles you have. Your phenotype is what characteristics you have.

## Genetic Diagrams Show the Possible Alleles of Offspring

Suppose you start breeding crazy hamsters. The allele which causes the crazy nature is recessive ("b"), whilst normal (boring) behaviour is due to a dominant allele ("B").

1) A crazy hamster must have the genotype bb. But a normal hamster could be BB or Bb.

2) Here's what happens if you breed from two homozygous hamsters:

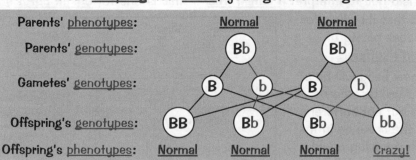

*genotype = BB or Bb*
*phenotype = normal*

| Parents' phenotypes: | Normal | Crazy |
|---|---|---|
| Parents' genotypes: | BB | bb |
| Gametes' genotypes: | B   B | b   b |
| Offspring's genotypes: | Bb   Bb | Bb   Bb |
| Offspring's phenotypes: | All the offspring are normal (boring). | |

*When you cross two parents to look at just one characteristic, it's called a monohybrid cross.*

3) If two of these offspring now breed, you'll get the next generation:

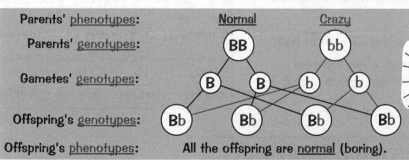

| Parents' phenotypes: | Normal | Normal |
|---|---|---|
| Parents' genotypes: | Bb | Bb |
| Gametes' genotypes: | B   b | B   b |
| Offspring's genotypes: | BB   Bb | Bb   bb |
| Offspring's phenotypes: | Normal   Normal | Normal   Crazy! |

*But remember — genetic diagrams only tell you probabilities, they don't say definitely what'll happen.*

4) That's a 3:1 ratio of normal to crazy offspring in this generation (a 1 in 4 or 25% probability of craziness).

## What do you get if you cross a kangaroo and a sheep...

...a ratio of 1:1 kangsheep to sheeparoos... bet you thought I was going to say a woolly jumper. In the exam you might be given the results of a breeding experiment and asked to say whether a characteristic is dominant or recessive. Look at the ratios of the characteristic in the different generations to help you work it out.

# More Genetic Diagrams

You've got to be able to <u>predict</u> and <u>explain</u> the outcomes of crosses between individuals for each <u>possible</u> <u>combination</u> of <u>dominant</u> and <u>recessive alleles</u> of a gene. You should be able to draw a <u>genetic diagram</u> and <u>work it out</u> — but it'll be easier if you've seen them all before. So here are a couple more examples for you. You also need to know how to interpret another type of genetic diagram called a <u>family tree</u>...

## All the Offspring are Normal

Let's take another look at the <u>crazy hamster</u> example from page 71:

In this cross, a hamster with <u>two</u> dominant alleles (BB) is crossed with a hamster with <u>two recessive alleles</u> (bb). <u>All</u> the offspring are normal (boring).

But, if you crossed a hamster with <u>two</u> dominant alleles (BB) with a hamster with <u>a dominant</u> and <u>a recessive allele</u> (Bb), you would also get <u>all</u> normal (boring) offspring.

To find out <u>which</u> it was you'd have to <u>breed the offspring together</u> and see what kind of <u>ratio</u> you got that time — then you'd have a good idea. If it was <u>3:1</u>, it's likely that you originally had BB and bb.

## There's a 1:1 Ratio in the Offspring

A cat with <u>long hair</u> was bred with another cat with <u>short hair</u>. The long hair is caused by a <u>dominant</u> allele 'H', and the short hair by a <u>recessive</u> allele 'h'.

They had 8 kittens — 4 with long hair and 4 with short hair.

This is a <u>1:1</u> ratio — it's what you'd expect when a parent with only <u>one dominant allele</u> (Hh) is crossed with a parent with <u>two recessive alleles</u> (hh).

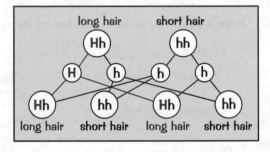

## You Need to be Able to Interpret Family Trees

Knowing how inheritance works can help you to interpret a <u>family tree</u> — this is one for <u>cystic fibrosis</u> (p. 73).

1) From the family tree, you can tell that the allele for cystic fibrosis <u>isn't</u> dominant because plenty of the family <u>carry</u> the allele but <u>aren't sufferers</u>.

2) There is a <u>25%</u> chance that the new baby will be a sufferer and a <u>50%</u> chance that it will be a carrier, as both of its parents are carriers but not sufferers. The case of the new baby is just the same as in the genetic diagram on page 73 — so the baby could be <u>normal</u> (FF), a <u>carrier</u> (Ff) or a <u>sufferer</u> (ff).

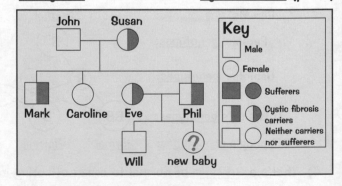

## It's enough to make you go cross-eyed...

In the exam you might get a <u>family tree</u> showing the inheritance of a <u>dominant allele</u> — in this case there won't be any carriers shown. Also, remember that a good way to work out a family tree is to write the <u>genotype</u> of each person onto it — you can practice by copying the family tree above and labelling the genotypes of everyone on it.

# Genetic Disorders

It's not just characteristics that are passed on — some <u>disorders</u> are inherited.  You need to <u>learn these ones</u>.

## Cystic Fibrosis is Caused by a Recessive Allele

<u>Cystic fibrosis</u> is a <u>genetic disorder</u> of the <u>cell membranes</u>.  It <u>results</u> in the body
producing a lot of thick sticky <u>mucus</u> in the <u>air passages</u> and in the <u>pancreas</u>.

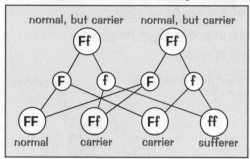

1) The allele which causes cystic fibrosis is a <u>recessive allele</u>, 'f', carried by about <u>1 person in 25</u>.

2) Because it's recessive, people with only <u>one copy</u> of the allele <u>won't</u> have the disorder — they're known as <u>carriers</u>.

3) For a child to have the disorder, <u>both parents</u> must be either <u>carriers</u> or <u>sufferers</u>.

4) As the diagram shows, there's a <u>1 in 4 chance</u> of a child having the disorder if <u>both</u> parents are <u>carriers</u>.

## Polydactyly is Caused by a Dominant Allele

<u>Polydactyly</u> is a <u>genetic disorder</u> where a baby's born with <u>extra fingers or toes</u>.
It doesn't usually cause any other problems so <u>isn't life-threatening</u>.

1) The disorder is caused by a <u>dominant allele</u>, 'D', and so can be inherited if just <u>one parent</u> carries the defective allele.

2) The <u>parent</u> that <u>has</u> the defective allele will be a <u>sufferer</u> too since the allele is dominant.

3) As the genetic diagram shows, there's a <u>50% chance</u> of a child having the disorder if <u>one</u> parent has the D allele.

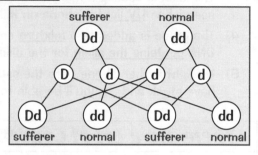

## Sickle-Cell Anaemia is Also Caused by a Recessive Allele

Sickle-cell anaemia is a <u>genetic disorder</u> characterised by funny-shaped red blood cells.
These red blood cells can get <u>stuck</u> in the capillaries, which <u>deprives</u> body cells of <u>oxygen</u>.
<u>Symptoms</u> include tiredness, painful joints and muscles, fever and anaemia.

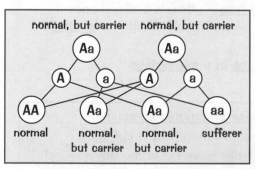

1) It's caused by inheriting two <u>recessive</u> alleles (a or Hb$^S$). The <u>dominant</u> normal allele is represented by A or Hb$^A$.

2) If two people who <u>carry</u> the sickle-cell anaemia allele have children, the <u>probability</u> of each child suffering from the disorder is 1 in 4 — <u>25%</u>.

If you <u>carry</u> the sickle-cell allele (heterozygous Aa) you're <u>less likely</u> to get <u>malaria</u> than if you're <u>homozygous</u> for the dominant allele (AA).  So if malaria is <u>very common</u> where you live (e.g. parts of Africa) being a <u>carrier</u> has some <u>benefits</u>.  Over time, this <u>advantage</u> has led to <u>more carriers</u> in areas where malaria is present.

## Some Disorders are Caused by the Wrong Number of Chromosomes

1) People <u>usually</u> have <u>23 pairs</u> of chromosomes — that's <u>46</u> chromosomes in total.

2) But some <u>disorders</u> are caused by <u>inheriting too few</u> or <u>too many chromosomes</u>.

3) <u>Down's Syndrome</u> is a <u>disorder</u> caused by the inheritance of an <u>extra chromosome</u>.  People with Down's Syndrome have <u>47 chromosomes</u> instead of 46, which can cause a variety of health issues.

## Unintentional mooning — caused by faulty jeans...

We <u>all</u> have defective genes in us somewhere.  Usually they don't cause a problem though as they're often <u>recessive</u>, and so if you have a healthy <u>dominant</u> allele too, you'll be fine.

# Embryo Screening

If a baby's at <u>risk</u> of having a <u>genetic disorder</u> (e.g. if both parents carry the recessive cystic fibrosis allele) then it can be <u>tested</u> for that <u>disorder</u> before it's born.  But there are <u>arguments</u> <u>for</u> and <u>against</u> doing this...

## Embryos Can Be Screened for Genetic Disorders

1) During <u>in vitro fertilisation</u> (IVF), embryos are fertilised in a <u>laboratory</u>, and then <u>implanted</u> into the mother's womb.  <u>More</u> than one egg is fertilised, so there's a better chance of the IVF being <u>successful</u>.

2) Before being implanted, it's possible to <u>remove a cell</u> from each embryo and <u>analyse</u> its <u>genes</u>.

3) Many <u>genetic disorders</u> could be <u>detected</u> in this way, such as cystic fibrosis.

4) It's also possible to get DNA from an embryo <u>in the womb</u> and test that for disorders.

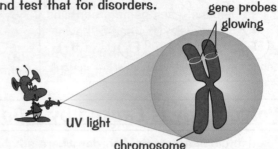

Here's how the test works:

1) <u>DNA</u> is <u>isolated</u> from the embryo's <u>cells</u>.

2) A <u>gene probe</u> is produced that will <u>bind</u> to the <u>allele</u> for a <u>specific disorder</u>.  (A gene probe is a <u>short section</u> of DNA that will bind to the allele for the disorder).

3) The probe is also <u>labelled</u> so that it can be <u>detected</u>. The label is usually a <u>fluorescent chemical</u> that can be seen when <u>UV light</u> is shone on it.

4) The probe is <u>added</u> to a <u>mixture</u> containing the <u>DNA sample</u> from the embryo.  If the embryo's DNA <u>contains the allele</u> for the disorder, the <u>probe</u> will <u>bind</u> to it.

5) UV light is then <u>shone</u> onto the <u>sample</u> — if the allele for the disorder is there, the <u>probe</u> will have stuck and so you'll be able to see it <u>glowing</u>.

## There are a Lot of Concerns about Embryonic Screening

You need to understand the concerns and issues raised by embryonic screening:

1) Embryonic screening is quite <u>controversial</u> because of the <u>decisions</u> it can lead to.

2) For embryos produced by <u>IVF</u> — after screening only embryos with '<u>good</u>' alleles would be <u>implanted</u> into the mother and the ones with '<u>bad</u>' alleles would be <u>destroyed</u>.

3) For embryos in the <u>womb</u> — screening could lead to the decision to <u>terminate</u> the pregnancy.

4) Screening is good but it <u>doesn't get the right answer 100% of the time</u> — there's a slim chance it might say that an embryo has a disorder when it actually doesn't — so it could result in a <u>healthy</u> embryo being terminated or destroyed by <u>mistake</u>.

5) <u>Taking cells</u> from embryos in the <u>womb</u> can also <u>increase</u> the <u>chance</u> of a <u>miscarriage</u>.

Here are some <u>more</u> arguments <u>for</u> and <u>against</u> screening.

| <u>Against Embryonic Screening</u> | <u>For Embryonic Screening</u> |
|---|---|
| 1) It implies that <u>people</u> with <u>genetic problems</u> are 'undesirable' — this could increase <u>prejudice</u>. | 1) It will help to stop people <u>suffering</u>. |
| 2) There may come a point where everyone wants to screen their embryos so they can pick the most '<u>desirable</u>' one, e.g. they want a blue-eyed, blond-haired, intelligent boy. | 2) Treating disorders costs the Government (and the taxpayers) a lot of <u>money</u>. |
| 3) Screening is <u>expensive</u>. | 3) There are <u>laws</u> to stop it going too far. At the moment parents cannot even select the sex of their baby (unless it's for health reasons). |

Many people think that embryonic screening <u>isn't justified</u> for genetic disorders that <u>don't</u> affect a person's health, such as <u>polydactyly</u>.

## Embryonic screening — it's a tricky one...

In the exam you may be asked to <u>compare</u> the issues <u>for</u> and <u>against</u> embryonic screening for <u>different disorders</u>. So make sure you can apply the <u>pros</u> and <u>cons</u> listed above to different disorders and you'll be sorted.

# Reproduction

Ooo err, reproduction... Surely you knew it'd come up at some point. It can happen in <u>two different ways</u>...

## Sexual Reproduction Produces Genetically Different Cells

1) <u>Sexual reproduction</u> is where genetic information from <u>two</u> organisms (a <u>father</u> and a <u>mother</u>) is combined to produce offspring which are <u>genetically different</u> to either parent.

Have a squizz at page 24 for the details of <u>meiosis</u>.

2) In sexual reproduction the mother and father produce <u>gametes</u> by <u>meiosis</u>. In <u>animals</u> meiosis produces <u>egg</u> (female gamete) and <u>sperm</u> (male gamete) cells.

3) In humans, each gamete contains <u>23 chromosomes</u> — <u>half</u> the number of chromosomes in a normal cell. (Instead of having <u>two</u> of each chromosome, a <u>gamete</u> has just <u>one</u> of each.)

4) The <u>egg</u> (from the mother) and the <u>sperm</u> cell (from the father) then <u>fuse together</u> (<u>fertilisation</u>) to form a cell with the <u>full number</u> of chromosomes (<u>half from the father</u>, <u>half from the mother</u>).

> <u>SEXUAL REPRODUCTION</u> involves the fusion of male and female gametes.
> Because there are <u>TWO</u> parents, the offspring contain <u>a mixture of their parents' genes</u>.

Fertilisation: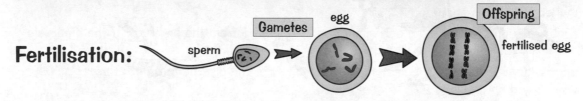

5) This is why the offspring <u>inherits features</u> from <u>both parents</u> — it's received a <u>mixture</u> of chromosomes from its mum and its dad (and it's the chromosomes that decide how you turn out).

6) This <u>mixture of genetic material</u> produces <u>variation</u> in the offspring — like different eye or hair colour, or a preference for eighties guitar music. (OK so I made the last one up — but my dad always says I didn't get my music taste from him).

## Asexual Reproduction Produces Genetically Identical Cells

1) In <u>asexual reproduction</u> there's only <u>one parent</u> so the offspring are <u>genetically identical</u> to that parent.

2) Asexual reproduction happens by <u>mitosis</u> — an <u>ordinary cell</u> makes a new cell by <u>dividing in two</u> (see page 23).

3) The <u>new cell</u> has <u>exactly the same</u> genetic information (i.e. genes) as the parent cell — it's called a <u>clone</u>.

> In <u>ASEXUAL REPRODUCTION</u> there's only <u>ONE</u> parent. There's <u>no fusion</u> of gametes, <u>no mixing</u> of chromosomes and <u>no genetic variation</u> between parent and offspring. The offspring are <u>genetically identical</u> to the parent — they're <u>clones</u>.

4) <u>Bacteria</u>, <u>some plants</u> and <u>some animals</u> reproduce <u>asexually</u>.

A handsome bunch — even if I do say so myself...

## You need to reproduce these facts in the exam...

The main messages on this page are that: 1) <u>sexual</u> reproduction needs <u>two</u> parents and forms cells that are <u>genetically different</u> to the parents, so there's <u>lots</u> of genetic variation. And 2) <u>asexual</u> reproduction needs just <u>one</u> parent to make genetically <u>identical</u> cells (clones), so there's <u>no genetic variation</u> in the offspring.

# Cloning

We can clone plants and animals in <u>several different ways</u>.  Cool.  But some of them have potential problems...

## Plants Can Be Cloned by Tissue Culture

This is where <u>a few plant cells</u> are put in a <u>growth medium</u> with <u>hormones</u>, and they grow into <u>new plants</u> — <u>clones</u> of the parent plant.  These plants can be made very <u>quickly</u>, in very little <u>space</u>, and be <u>grown all year</u>.

## You Can Make Animal Clones Using Embryo Transplants

Farmers can produce <u>cloned offspring</u> from their best bull and cow — using <u>embryo transplants</u>.

1) <u>Sperm cells</u> are taken from a prize bull and <u>egg cells</u> are taken from a prize cow.
   The sperm are then used to <u>artificially fertilise</u> an egg cell.  The <u>embryo</u> that develops
   is then <u>split</u> many times (to form <u>clones</u>) <u>before any cells</u> become <u>specialised</u>.

2) These <u>cloned embryos</u> can then be <u>implanted</u> into lots of other cows where
   they grow into <u>baby calves</u> (which will all be <u>genetically identical</u> to each other).

3) <u>Hundreds</u> of "ideal" offspring can be produced <u>every year</u> from the best bull and cow.

## Adult Cell Cloning is Another Way to Make a Clone

1) <u>Adult cell cloning</u> involves taking an unfertilised <u>egg cell</u> and removing its <u>genetic material</u>
   (the nucleus).  A <u>complete set</u> of <u>chromosomes</u> from an <u>adult body cell</u> (e.g. skin cell) is
   inserted into the 'empty' egg cell.

2) The egg cell is then stimulated by an <u>electric shock</u> — this makes it <u>divide</u>, just like a normal embryo.

3) When the embryo is a ball of cells, it's <u>implanted</u> into an <u>adult female</u> (the surrogate mother)
   to grow into a genetically identical copy (clone) of the original adult body cell.

4) This technique was used to create <u>Dolly</u> — the famous <u>cloned sheep</u>.

## There are Many Issues Surrounding Cloning

1) Cloning quickly gets you lots of "ideal" offspring.  But you also get a
   "<u>reduced gene pool</u>" — this means there are fewer different alleles in a population.
   If a population are all closely <u>related</u> and a new disease appears, they could all be
   <u>wiped out</u> — there may be no allele in the population giving <u>resistance</u> to the disease.

2) But the <u>study</u> of animal clones could lead to greater <u>understanding</u> of the
   development of the <u>embryo</u>, and of <u>ageing</u> and <u>age-related disorders</u>.

3) Cloning could also be used to help preserve <u>endangered species</u>.

4) However, it's possible that cloned animals might <u>not</u> be as <u>healthy</u> as normal ones, e.g. Dolly the sheep
   had <u>arthritis</u>, which tends to occur in <u>older sheep</u> (but the jury's still out on if this was due to cloning).

5) Some people worry that <u>humans</u> might be cloned in the future.  If it was allowed, any <u>success</u> may follow
   <u>many unsuccessful attempts</u>, e.g. children born severely disabled.

**Egg cell**

**Adult body cell**

**Nucleus removed**

**Nucleus removed**

**Electric shock**

**Embryo**

**Implanted into surrogate mother**

**Live animal**

## Thank goodness they didn't do that with my little brother...

Cloning can be a <u>controversial</u> topic — especially when it's to do with cloning animals (and especially humans).
More <u>large-scale</u>, <u>long-term studies</u> into cloned animals are needed to find out what the <u>dangers</u> are.

# Genetic Engineering

Scientists can now <u>change</u> an organism's <u>genes</u> to alter its characteristics.
This is a fairly new science with exciting possibilities, but there are <u>concerns</u> too, of course...

## Genetic Engineering Uses Enzymes to Cut and Paste Genes

The basic idea is to copy a <u>useful gene</u> (section of DNA) from one organism's chromosome into another...

1) A useful gene is "<u>cut</u>" from one organism's chromosome using <u>enzymes</u>.

2) This gene is <u>inserted</u> into a <u>vector</u> — usually a <u>virus</u> (which inserts its DNA into the organism it infects) or a <u>bacterial plasmid</u> (a <u>small ring</u> of DNA that can be passed between bacteria).

3) The <u>vector</u> is then used to <u>insert</u> the gene into a different organism, or into the <u>chromosome</u> of the different organism. The DNA is used to make a <u>protein</u> (see p. 68).

4) Scientists use this method to do all sorts of things — for example, the human insulin gene can be inserted into <u>bacteria</u> to <u>produce human insulin</u>:

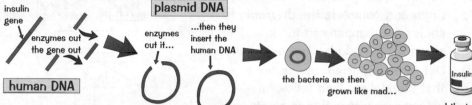

insulin gene

enzymes cut the gene out

human DNA

plasmid DNA

enzymes cut it...

...then they insert the human DNA

the bacteria are then grown like mad...

Insulin

...and the insulin produced is purified and used by people with diabetes.

## Genes can be Transferred into Animals and Plants

The same method can be used to <u>transfer useful genes</u> into <u>animals</u> and <u>plants</u> at the <u>very early stages</u> of their development (i.e. shortly after <u>fertilisation</u>). This means they'll develop <u>useful characteristics</u>.
<u>Genetically modified</u> (<u>GM</u>) <u>crops</u> are crop plants that have had their genes modified, e.g. to make them <u>resistant to viruses</u>, <u>insect attacks</u> or <u>herbicides</u> (chemicals used to kill weeds).

## But Genetic Engineering is a Controversial Topic...

1) Genetic engineering is an <u>exciting new area in science</u> which has the <u>potential</u> for solving many of our problems (e.g. treating diseases, more efficient food production etc.) but not everyone thinks it's a great idea.

2) There are <u>worries</u> about the long-term effects of genetic engineering — that changing a person's genes might <u>accidentally</u> create unplanned <u>problems</u>, which could then get passed on to <u>future generations</u>.

### It's the Same with GM Crops — There are Pros and Cons...

1) Some people say that growing GM crops will affect the number of <u>weeds</u> and <u>flowers</u> (and so the population of <u>insects</u>) that live in and around the crops — <u>reducing</u> farmland <u>biodiversity</u>.

2) Not everyone is convinced that GM crops are <u>safe</u>. People are worried they may develop <u>allergies</u> to the food — although there's probably no more risk for this than for eating usual foods.

3) A big concern is that <u>transplanted genes</u> may get out into the <u>natural environment</u>. For example, the <u>herbicide resistance</u> gene may be picked up by weeds, creating a new '<u>superweed</u>' variety.

4) On the plus side, GM crops can <u>increase the yield</u> of a crop, making more food.

5) People living in developing nations often lack <u>nutrients</u> in their diets. GM crops could be <u>engineered</u> to contain the nutrient that's <u>missing</u>. For example, they're testing 'golden rice' that contains beta-carotene — lack of this substance causes <u>blindness</u>.

6) GM crops are already being grown elsewhere in the world (not the UK) often <u>without any problems</u>.

I say it's great.

## If only there was a gene to make revision easier...

At the end of the day, it's up to the <u>Government</u> to weigh up all the <u>evidence</u> for the pros and cons before <u>making a decision</u> on how this scientific knowledge is used. All scientists can do is make sure the Government has all the information it needs to make the decision. And all you need to do is to <u>learn</u> this page inside out.

# Revision Summary for Section Seven

Wow, that was a packed section. All that geneticsy stuff can take a while to get your head round — so here are some questions to help you do just that. If there are any questions you don't know the answer to, look back and learn those bits again. Then try the questions again, and again...

1) Name three animal characteristics that are determined a) only by genes, b) by a mixture of genes and the environment.
2) What does DNA stand for?
3) Where in the cell do you find chromosomes?
4) What does the order of bases in a gene code for?
5) How many pairs of chromosomes do humans have in each cell?
6) Which sex chromosomes do males have?
7) Copy and complete the diagrams to show what happens to the X and Y chromosomes during reproduction.

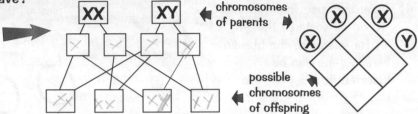

8) List three important conclusions that Mendel reached following his experiments with pea plants.
9) What is an allele?
10) What is meant by an organism being heterozygous? What about homozygous?
11) Describe the basic difference between a recessive allele and a dominant one.
12)* Blue colour in a plant is carried on a recessive allele, b. The dominant allele, B, gives white flowers. In the first generation after a cross, all the flowers are white. These are bred together and the result is a ratio of 54 white : 19 blue. What were the alleles of the flowers used in the first cross?
13) If both parents carry one recessive allele for cystic fibrosis, what is the probability of their child being a carrier?
14) What is polydactyly?
15) Why might it be an advantage to carry one copy of the recessive allele for sickle-cell anaemia?
16) Explain how embryos are screened for genetic disorders.
17) Why are some people concerned about embryo screening?
18) The table below compares sexual and asexual reproduction.
Complete the table by ticking whether each statement is true for sexual or asexual reproduction.

|  | Sexual reproduction | Asexual reproduction |
|---|---|---|
| Reproduction involves two parents. |  |  |
| Offspring are clones of the parent. |  |  |
| There is variation in the offspring. |  |  |
| There is no fusion of gametes. |  |  |

19) How would you make a plant clone using tissue culture?
20) Why are some people concerned about genetic engineering?

* Answer on page 100.

*Section Seven — Variation and Genetics*

# Adaptations

Organisms survive in many <u>different environments</u> because they have <u>adapted</u> to them.

## Adaptations allow Organisms to Survive

<u>Organisms</u>, and <u>microorganisms</u>, are <u>adapted</u> to live in certain environmental <u>conditions</u>. The <u>features</u> or <u>characteristics</u> that allow them to do this are called <u>adaptations</u>. Adaptations can be:

**STRUCTURAL** These are <u>features</u> of an organism's <u>body structure</u> — such as <u>shape</u> or <u>colour</u>. E.g. <u>Arctic</u> animals like <u>polar bears</u> have <u>white fur</u> so they're <u>camouflaged</u> against the snow. This helps them <u>avoid predators</u> and <u>sneak up on prey</u>. Animals that live in <u>cold</u> places (like <u>whales</u>) have a <u>thick layer</u> of <u>blubber</u> (fat) and a <u>low surface area to volume ratio</u> to help them <u>retain heat</u>. Animals that live in <u>hot</u> places (like <u>camels</u>) have a thin layer of fat and a <u>large surface area to volume ratio</u> to help them <u>lose heat</u>.

**BEHAVIOURAL** These are ways that organisms <u>behave</u>. Many species (e.g. <u>reindeer</u> or <u>swallows</u>) <u>migrate</u> to <u>warmer climates</u> during the <u>winter</u> to <u>avoid</u> the problems of living in <u>cold conditions</u>.

**FUNCTIONAL** These are things that go on <u>inside</u> an organism's <u>body</u> that can be <u>related</u> to <u>processes</u> like <u>reproduction</u> and <u>metabolism</u>. E.g. <u>Brown bears hibernate</u> over <u>winter</u>. They <u>lower their metabolism</u> (all the chemical reactions happening in their body) which <u>conserves energy</u>, so they <u>don't have to hunt</u> when there's <u>not much food</u> about. <u>Desert</u> animals <u>conserve water</u> by producing <u>very little sweat</u> and <u>small amounts</u> of <u>concentrated urine</u>.

## Microorganisms Have a Huge Variety of Adaptations...

...so that they can live in a <u>wide range</u> of environments:

Some <u>microorganisms</u> (e.g. bacteria) are known as <u>extremophiles</u> — they're adapted to live in seriously <u>extreme conditions</u> like super <u>hot</u> volcanic vents, in very <u>salty</u> lakes or at <u>high pressure</u> on the sea bed.

## Parasites are Adapted to Live On or Inside their Hosts

Parasitic organisms <u>depend</u> on <u>other species</u> to survive. You need to <u>learn</u> these <u>two</u> examples:

**FLEAS** Fleas live in the <u>hair</u> or <u>fur</u> of <u>mammals</u> and <u>suck blood</u> from their host. They are <u>adapted</u> to this environment by having:

1) <u>Sharp mouthparts</u> to help them <u>break</u> the host's <u>skin</u> and <u>suck blood</u>.
2) A <u>flattened body</u> so they're <u>not</u> easily <u>brushed off</u> their host.
3) A <u>hard body</u> so they're <u>not damaged</u> when the animal <u>scratches</u> at them.
4) <u>Long hind (back) legs</u> so they can <u>jump between</u> hosts.

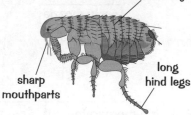

hard, flattened body

long hind legs

sharp mouthparts

(Not to scale — that would be scary!)

**TAPEWORMS** Tapeworms live in the <u>intestines</u> of <u>mammals</u> and some <u>other animals</u>. They are <u>adapted</u> to this environment by having:

1) <u>Suckers</u> and <u>hooks</u> to help them <u>hold on</u> to the <u>wall</u> of the host's <u>intestine</u>.
2) A <u>body</u> with <u>flattened segments</u> and <u>no gut</u>. The body has a <u>large surface area</u> so it can <u>absorb its food</u> from the <u>host's gut</u>. The flattened segments produce <u>a lot of eggs</u> so the tapeworm can have lots of <u>babies</u> (cute).
3) A <u>thick outer cuticle</u> (skin) to <u>stop</u> them getting <u>digested</u> by the <u>enzymes</u> in the host's gut (along with the rest of the host's dinner — <u>yum</u>).

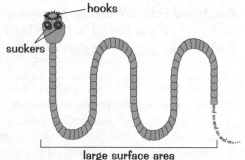

hooks

suckers

and on and on and on....

large surface area

## In a nutshell, it's horses for courses...

In the exam, you might have to say how an organism is adapted to its environment. Look at its <u>characteristics</u> (e.g. <u>colour/shape</u>) as well as the <u>conditions</u> it has to cope with (e.g. <u>predation/temperature</u>) and you'll be sorted.

# The Malaria Parasite

The <u>malaria parasite</u> is a very <u>clever</u> but rather <u>nasty</u> little critter.  Read on to find out why...

## The Malaria Parasite is a Single-Celled Organism

1) <u>Malaria</u> in <u>humans</u> is caused by the <u>single-celled malaria parasite</u>.
2) The parasite's <u>complex life cycle</u> takes place <u>partly</u> in <u>animals</u> (including <u>humans</u>) and <u>partly</u> in <u>mosquitos</u>.
3) Mosquitos <u>don't cause</u> malaria, they just <u>pass on</u> the <u>parasite</u> as they <u>bite</u> animals to <u>feed</u> on their <u>blood</u>.
4) The parasite takes a <u>different form</u> in each <u>different stage</u> of its life cycle.
5) <u>Each form</u> is adapted for living in a <u>different place</u> in the <u>animal or mosquito host</u>.

## The Four Different Forms of the Malaria Parasite

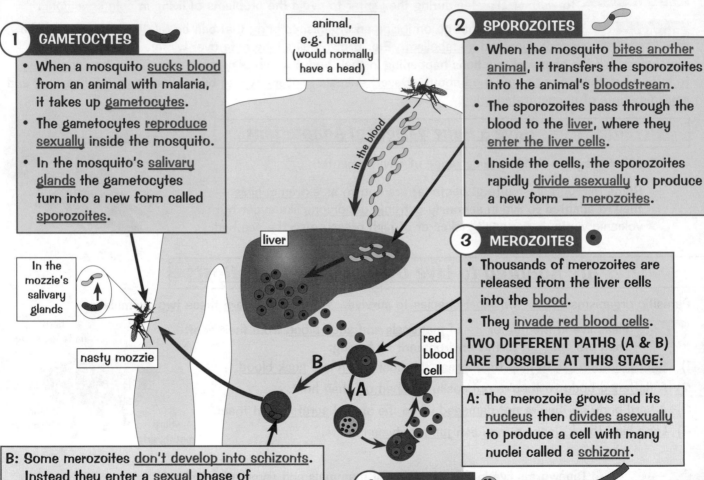

**1 GAMETOCYTES**

- When a mosquito <u>sucks blood</u> from an animal with malaria, it takes up <u>gametocytes</u>.
- The gametocytes <u>reproduce sexually</u> inside the mosquito.
- In the mosquito's <u>salivary glands</u> the gametocytes turn into a new form called <u>sporozoites</u>.

In the mozzie's salivary glands

nasty mozzie

animal, e.g. human (would normally have a head)

in the blood

liver

**2 SPOROZOITES**

- When the mosquito <u>bites another animal</u>, it transfers the sporozoites into the animal's <u>bloodstream</u>.
- The sporozoites pass through the blood to the <u>liver</u>, where they <u>enter the liver cells</u>.
- Inside the cells, the sporozoites rapidly <u>divide asexually</u> to produce a new form — <u>merozoites</u>.

**3 MEROZOITES**

- Thousands of merozoites are released from the liver cells into the <u>blood</u>.
- They <u>invade red blood cells</u>.

**TWO DIFFERENT PATHS (A & B) ARE POSSIBLE AT THIS STAGE:**

**A:** The merozoite grows and its <u>nucleus</u> then <u>divides asexually</u> to produce a cell with many nuclei called a <u>schizont</u>.

red blood cell

B     A

**B:** Some merozoites <u>don't develop into schizonts</u>. Instead they enter a <u>sexual</u> phase of reproduction which results in <u>gametocytes</u>. Red blood cells containing gametocytes can be <u>sucked up</u> if the animal is bitten by a <u>mosquito</u>. And so the <u>life cycle</u> begins all over <u>again</u>.

**4 SCHIZONTS**

- The schizont <u>divides</u> to produce many <u>merozoites</u> (each merozoite only has <u>one</u> nucleus).
- The red blood cell <u>bursts</u>, releasing merozoites into the blood.  <u>Toxins</u> are released too, <u>triggering</u> the <u>fever attacks</u> that are associated with malaria.
- These merozoites go on to <u>invade</u> other red blood cells and the <u>cycle is repeated</u>.
- Infected red blood cells all tend to burst <u>at the same time</u> — the <u>cycles</u> of bursting cells results in the <u>cycles</u> of <u>fever attacks</u> malaria victims get.

The parasite has lots of different adaptations — for example:
- Merozoites have sticky protein molecules on their surface that help them 'catch' a red blood cell so they can invade it. They are also very small, making invasion easier.
- In animals the parasites are adapted to live inside cells, meaning it is hard for the immune system to detect and destroy them.

## GAMEs & SPORts or MERingues & SCHnapps..?

OK it's a bit of a pants way to remember the <u>four life stages</u> — but however you do it, you need to <u>learn 'em</u>.

# Competition and Environmental Change

It's tough in the wild — there's always <u>competition</u> for <u>food</u> and <u>other resources</u>. So if the <u>environment</u> <u>changes</u>, e.g. there's not enough food or it's too hot, that can be the last straw and <u>populations can decline</u>.

## Organisms Compete for Resources to Survive

Organisms need things from their <u>environment</u> and from <u>other organisms</u> in order to <u>survive</u> and <u>reproduce</u>:

1) <u>Plants</u> need <u>light</u>, <u>space</u>, <u>water</u> and <u>minerals (nutrients)</u> from the soil.

2) <u>Animals</u> need <u>space (territory)</u>, <u>food</u>, <u>water</u> and <u>mates</u>.

Organisms <u>compete with other species</u> (and members of their own species) for the <u>same resources</u>. E.g. red and grey <u>squirrels</u> live in the same habitat and eat the same food. Competition with the grey squirrels for these resources means there's not enough food for the reds — so the <u>population</u> of red squirrels is <u>decreasing</u>.

## Environmental Changes are Caused by Different Factors

The <u>environment</u> in which plants and animals live <u>changes all the time</u>. These changes are caused by <u>living</u> and <u>non-living</u> factors, such as:

> A change could be an increase or a decrease.

**LIVING FACTORS**  1) A change in the number or types of <u>competitors</u>.

**NON-LIVING FACTORS**
1) A change in average <u>temperature</u>.
2) A change in the availability of <u>nutrients</u>.
3) A change in the amount of <u>light</u>.
4) A change in average <u>rainfall</u> (and so how much <u>water</u> is available).
5) A change in the availability of <u>oxygen</u> and <u>carbon dioxide</u>.
6) A change in the availability of <u>nesting sites</u>, <u>shelter</u> and <u>habitats</u> (places to live).

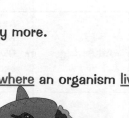

## Environmental Changes Affect Communities in Different Ways

Living organisms form <u>communities</u> — groups of <u>populations</u> of <u>different species</u> that <u>interact</u> with each other. Understanding the <u>relationships</u> <u>within</u> and <u>between</u> these communities can help us to see how they might be <u>affected</u> by <u>environmental changes</u>. Environmental changes can cause <u>population sizes</u> to <u>increase</u> or <u>decrease</u>, or cause the <u>distribution of organisms</u> to change:

**1) Population SIZE INCREASES**

E.g. if the number of <u>prey increases</u>, then there's <u>more food</u> available for predators, so more predators survive and reproduce, and their numbers <u>increase</u> too.

**2) Population SIZE DECREASES**

E.g. the number of bees in the US is <u>falling rapidly</u>.
Experts aren't sure why but they <u>think</u> it could be because:
1) Some <u>pesticides</u> may be having a negative effect on bees.
2) There's <u>less food</u> available — there aren't as many <u>nectar-rich plants</u> around any more.
3) There's <u>more disease</u> — bees are being killed by new pathogens or parasites.

**3) Population DISTRIBUTION CHANGES**  A change in distribution means a change in <u>where</u> an organism <u>lives</u>.

For example, the distribution of <u>bird species</u> in Germany is changing because of a rise in average <u>temperature</u>. E.g. the <u>European Bee-Eater</u> bird is a <u>Mediterranean</u> species but it's now present in parts of <u>Germany</u>.

---

## *I compete with my brother for the front seat of the car...*

In the exam you might be given some <u>data</u> and asked about the change in distribution of <u>any</u> organism. But don't panic — just think about what that organism would need to <u>survive</u> and any <u>environmental changes</u> that have occurred. And remember, if things are in <u>limited supply</u> then there's going to be <u>competition</u>.

# Measuring Environmental Change

It's difficult to measure accurately just how much our environment is changing. But there are some useful indicators that can be used...

## Environmental Changes can be Measured Using Living Indicators...

1) Some organisms are very sensitive to changes in their environment and so can be studied to see the effect of human activities — these organisms are known as indicator species.

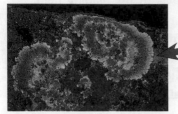

2) For example, air pollution can be monitored by looking at particular types of lichen that are very sensitive to the concentration of sulfur dioxide in the atmosphere (and so can give a good idea about the level of pollution from car exhausts, power stations, etc.). The number and type of lichen at a particular location will indicate how clean the air is (e.g. the air is clean if there are lots of lichen).

3) If raw sewage is released into a river, the bacterial population in the water increases and uses up the oxygen. Some invertebrate animals, like mayfly larvae, are good indicators for water pollution because they're very sensitive to the concentration of dissolved oxygen in the water. If you find mayfly larvae in a river, it indicates that the water is clean.

4) Other invertebrate species have adapted to live in polluted conditions — so if you see a lot of them you know there's a problem. E.g. rat-tailed maggots and sludgeworms indicate a very high level of water pollution.

## ...and Non-Living Indicators

Environmental change can also be measured using non-living indicators like oxygen levels, temperature and rainfall. Scientists use lots of clever equipment to do this. For example:

1) Satellites measure the temperature of the sea surface. They are modern, accurate instruments and give us a global coverage.

2) Automatic weather stations tell us the atmospheric temperature at various locations. They contain sensitive and accurate thermometers that can measure to very small fractions of a degree.

3) Rain gauges measure rainfall, to see how much the average rainfall changes year on year.

4) Dissolved oxygen meters measure the concentration of dissolved oxygen in water, to discover how the level of water pollution is changing.

## Both Ways of Looking at Environmental Change Have Their Weaknesses

Here are a few examples of the advantages and disadvantages of using living and non-living indicators to measure environmental change. You might be able to think of some more.

|  | Living methods (indicator species) | Non-living methods (using equipment) |
|---|---|---|
| Advantages | • A relatively quick, cheap and easy way of seeing whether an area is polluted or not.<br>• Gives a long term view rather than a snapshot, because populations of organisms change relatively slowly as the environment changes. | • Directly measuring pollutants or non-living indicators of environmental change gives reliable, numerical data that's easy to compare between different sites.<br>• The exact pollutants can be identified and their concentrations measured. |
| Disadvantages | • Using indicator species to measure pollution isn't always reliable because their survival can be affected by other factors (e.g. temperature). | • Requires expensive equipment (satellites etc.).<br>• Trained workers are needed to operate the equipment.<br>• Only gives a snapshot of conditions at the time the measurements were taken. |

## Teenagers are an indicator species — not found in clean rooms...

Recording the levels of living and non-living things helps scientists to see how our environment is changing. In the exam, you might get some data about pollution — you'll have to figure out what the data means, and the pros and cons of the method used to measure the pollution. So you'd best learn this page.

# Monitoring the Distribution of Organisms

This is where the <u>fun</u> starts.  Studying <u>ecology</u> gives you the chance to <u>rummage around</u> in bushes, get your hands <u>dirty</u> and look at some <u>real organisms</u>, living in the <u>wild</u>.  Hold on to your hats folks...

## Organisms Live in Different Places Because The Environment Varies

1) A <u>habitat</u> is the place where an organism <u>lives</u>, e.g. a playing field.

2) The <u>distribution</u> of an organism is <u>where</u> an organism is <u>found</u>, e.g. in a part of the playing field.

3) Where an organism is found is affected by <u>environmental factors</u> (see page 81).  An organism might be <u>more common</u> in <u>one area</u> than another due to <u>differences</u> in environmental factors between the two areas.  For example, in the playing field, you might find that daisies are <u>more common</u> in the open than under trees, because there's <u>more light</u> available in the open.

4) There are a couple of ways to <u>study</u> the distribution of an organism.  You can:

 • <u>measure</u> how common an organism is in <u>two sample areas</u> (e.g. using <u>quadrats</u>) and compare them.
 • study how the distribution <u>changes</u> across an area, e.g. by placing quadrats along a <u>transect</u> (p. 84).
 Both of these methods give <u>quantitative</u> data (numbers) about the distribution.

## Use Quadrats to Study The Distribution of Small Organisms

A <u>quadrat</u> is a <u>square</u> frame enclosing a <u>known area</u>, e.g. 1 m². To compare <u>how common</u> an organism is in <u>two sample areas</u> (e.g. shady and sunny spots in that playing field) just follow these simple steps:

1) Place a <u>1 m² quadrat</u> on the ground at a <u>random point</u> within the <u>first</u> sample area.
 E.g. divide the area into a grid and use a random number generator to pick coordinates.

2) <u>Count</u> all the organisms <u>within</u> the quadrat.

3) <u>Repeat</u> steps 1 and 2 as many times as you can.

4) <u>Work out</u> the <u>mean</u> number of organisms per quadrat within the first sample area.

A quadrat

> • For example, Anna counted the number of daisies in 7 quadrats within her first sample area and recorded the following results: 18, 20, 22, 23, 23, 23, 25
>
> • Here the MEAN is:  $\dfrac{\text{TOTAL number of organisms}}{\text{NUMBER of quadrats}} = \dfrac{154}{7} = \underline{22}$ daisies per quadrat.
>
> • You also need to know about the MODE, which is the MOST COMMON value.  In this example it's <u>23</u>.
>
> • And the MEDIAN is the MIDDLE value, when they're in order of size.  In this example it's <u>23</u> also.

5) <u>Repeat</u> steps 1 to 4 in the <u>second</u> sample area.

6) Finally <u>compare</u> the two means.  E.g. you might find 2 daisies per m² in the shade, and 22 daisies per m² (lots more) in the open field.

### In the Exam You Might Have to Work Out Population Size

To work out the <u>population size</u> of an organism in one sample area:

1) Work out the <u>mean number of organisms per m²</u>.
 (If your quadrat has an area of 1 m², this is the <u>same</u> as the mean number of organisms per quadrat, worked out above.)

2) Then multiply the <u>mean</u> by the <u>total area</u> (in m²) of the habitat.

3) E.g. if the area of an open field is 800 m², and there are 22 daisies per m², then the size of the daisy population is 22 x 800 = 17 600.

Ben liked looking after his quad-rats.

## Drat, drat, and double drat — my favourite use of quadrats...

You must put your quadrat down in a <u>random place</u> before you start counting.  Anything, even chucking the quadrat over your shoulder*, is better than plonking it down right on the <u>first big patch</u> of organisms that you see.

*not an invitation to break equipment or maim fellow students etc.

# Monitoring the Distribution of Organisms

So, now you think you've learnt <u>all about</u> distribution. Well <u>hold on</u> — there's more <u>ecology fun</u> to be had.

## Use Transects to Study The Distribution of Organisms Along a Line

You can use lines called <u>transects</u> to help find out how organisms (like plants) are <u>distributed</u> across an area — e.g. if an organism becomes <u>more or less common</u> as you move from a hedge towards the middle of a field. Here's what to do:

1) <u>Mark out a line</u> in the area you want to study using a tape measure.

2) Then <u>collect data</u> along the line.

3) You can do this by just <u>counting</u> all the organisms you're interested in that <u>touch</u> the line.

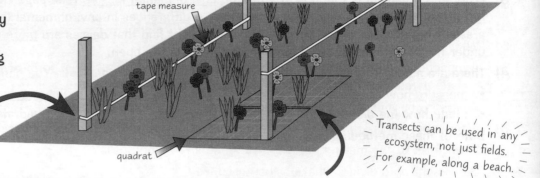

tape measure

quadrat

_Transects can be used in any ecosystem, not just fields. For example, along a beach._

4) Or, you can collect data by using <u>quadrats</u> (see previous page). These can be placed <u>next to</u> each other along the line or <u>at intervals</u>, for example, every 2 m.

## When Collecting Environmental Data You Need to Think About...

### ① Reproducibility and repeatability

1) <u>Quadrats</u> and <u>transects</u> are <u>pretty good tools</u> for finding out how an organism is distributed.

2) But, you have to work hard to make sure your results are <u>repeatable</u> (by you within the same experiment) and <u>reproducible</u> (other people can reproduce them).

3) Results are more likely to be reproducible if you use a <u>large sample size</u>, e.g. use as many quadrats and transects as possible in your sample area. Bigger samples are more <u>representative</u> of the whole population, so results using a larger sample are more likely to be <u>reproducible</u>.

### ② Validity

1) For your results to be <u>valid</u> they must be <u>repeatable</u>, <u>reproducible</u> and <u>answer the original question</u>.

2) To answer the original question, you need to <u>control all the variables</u>.

3) The question you want to answer is whether a <u>difference in distribution</u> between two sample areas is <u>due</u> to a <u>difference in one environmental factor</u>.

4) If you've controlled all the <u>other variables</u> that could be affecting the distribution, you'll know whether a <u>difference in distribution</u> is caused by the <u>environmental factor</u> or not.

5) If you <u>don't</u> control the other variables you <u>won't know</u> whether any correlation you've found is because of <u>chance</u>, because of the <u>environmental factor</u> you're looking at or because of a <u>different variable</u> — the study <u>won't give you valid data</u>.

6) Results are also more likely to be valid if you use <u>random</u> samples, e.g. randomly put down or mark out your quadrat or transect. If all your samples are in <u>one spot</u>, and everywhere else is <u>different</u>, the results you get won't be <u>valid</u>.

## A slug that's been run over — definitely a widely-spread organism...

In the exam, you may get the <u>results</u> of a study into the distribution of organisms and be asked questions on it. If you're asked to suggest <u>reasons</u> for the <u>distribution</u>, think about <u>environmental factors</u>. If you need to work out the <u>number of organisms per transect</u> just <u>take your time</u> and <u>check</u> your answer. If you're asked about <u>validity</u>, read the method carefully and think about the original question and the <u>samples taken</u>.

# Revision Summary for Section Eight

Well that section was short and sweet. But that doesn't mean it was easy — there's some complicated stuff to remember. So here are some questions to help you figure out what you know. If you get any wrong, go back and learn the stuff.

1) Name the three types of adaptation and give one example of each type.
2) Why do animals that live in the desert have a large surface area to volume ratio?
3) Give an example of a place where an extremophile might live.
4) Give two ways in which a flea is adapted to live on its host.
5) Why do tapeworms have a thick outer cuticle?
6) A mosquito sucks blood from a human infected with malaria. What form of the malaria parasite will the mosquito be infected by?
7) Where in the mosquito do gametocytes turn into sporozoites?
8) After sporozoites are passed into an animal by a mosquito bite, they travel to which organ?
9) What form of the malaria parasite first infects red blood cells?
10) When schizonts divide, what do they produce?
11) Name three things that: a) plants compete for, b) animals compete for.
12) Give three examples of non-living factors that can cause environmental changes.
13) Explain how lichen can be used as an indicator of air pollution.
14) Name an organism that can be used as an indicator of water pollution.
15) Give an example of a non-living indicator.
16) Give one advantage and one disadvantage of using living indicator species to measure pollution.
17) Give one advantage and one disadvantage of using equipment to measure non-living indicators of environmental change.
18) What is a habitat?
19) What is the distribution of an organism?
20) Briefly describe how you could find out how common an organism is in two sample areas using quadrats.
21) Describe one way of using a transect to find out how an organism is distributed across an area.
22) When you're collecting data about the distribution of organisms, why is it important to use a large sample size (e.g. several quadrats or transects)?

# Human Impact on the Environment

We have an impact on the world around us — and the more humans there are, the bigger the impact.

## There are Over Six Billion People in the World...

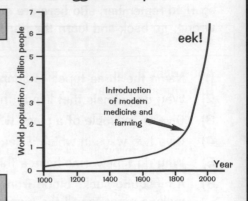

eek!

1) The population of the world is currently rising very quickly, and it's not slowing down — look at the graph...

2) This is mostly due to modern medicine and farming methods, which have reduced the number of people dying from disease and hunger.

3) This is great for all of us humans, but it means we're having a bigger effect on the environment we live in.

Introduction of modern medicine and farming

## ...With Increasing Demands on the Environment

When the Earth's population was much smaller, the effects of human activity were usually small and local. Nowadays though, our actions can have a far more widespread effect.

1) Our increasing population puts pressure on the environment, as we take the resources we need to survive.

2) But people around the world are also demanding a higher standard of living (and so demand luxuries to make life more comfortable — cars, computers, etc.). So we use more raw materials (e.g. oil to make plastics), but we also use more energy for the manufacturing processes. This all means we're taking more and more resources from the environment more and more quickly.

3) Unfortunately, many raw materials are being used up quicker than they're being replaced. So if we carry on like we are, one day we're going to run out.

## We're Also Producing More Waste

As we make more and more things we produce more and more waste. And unless this waste is properly handled, more harmful pollution will be caused. This affects water, land and air.

**Water** Sewage and toxic chemicals from industry can pollute lakes, rivers and oceans, affecting the plants and animals that rely on them for survival (including humans). And the chemicals used on land (e.g. fertilisers) can be washed into water. Sewage and fertilisers can cause eutrophication — see next page.

**Land** We use toxic chemicals for farming (e.g. pesticides and herbicides) — these can also get washed from land into water. We also bury nuclear waste underground, and we dump a lot of household waste in landfill sites.

**Air** Smoke and gases released into the atmosphere pollute the air, e.g. sulfur dioxide can cause acid rain.

## More People Means Less Land for Plants and Other Animals

Humans also reduce the amount of land and resources available to other animals and plants. The four main human activities that do this are:

| 1) Building | 2) Farming | 3) Dumping Waste | 4) Quarrying for metal ores |
|---|---|---|---|
|  |  |  |  |

## More people, more mess, less space, fewer resources...

Well, I don't know about you, but I feel just a little bit guilty. We're destroying the planet and all because there are loads more of us than there were before, and we're demanding a higher standard of living. In the exam you might be given some data about environmental impact to analyse, so make sure you understand what's going on.

# Eutrophication

I'm sorry to put so much gloom in such a short space, but you need to know more about pollution caused by waste fertilisers and sewage. Enjoy...

## Fertilisers can Leach into Water and Cause Eutrophication

You might think fertiliser would be a good thing for the environment because it makes plants grow faster. Unfortunately it causes big problems when it ends up in lakes and rivers — here's how...

1) Nitrates and phosphates are put onto fields as mineral fertilisers.

2) If too much fertiliser is applied and it rains afterwards, nitrates are easily leached (washed through the soil) into rivers and lakes.

3) The result is eutrophication, which can cause serious damage to rivers and lakes:

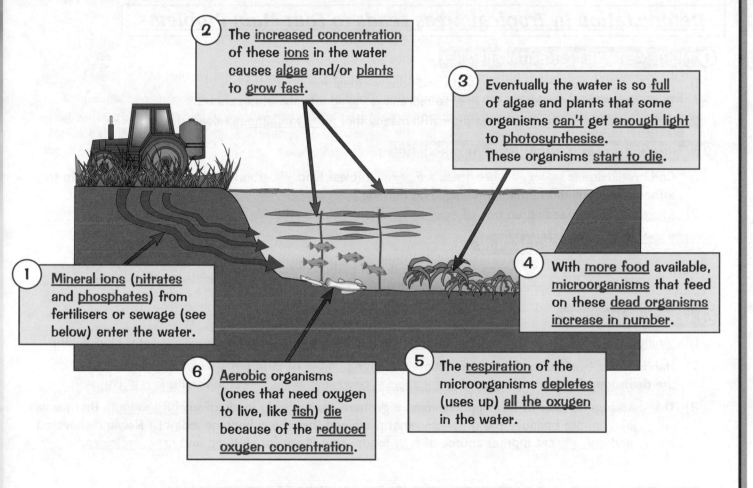

**2** The increased concentration of these ions in the water causes algae and/or plants to grow fast.

**3** Eventually the water is so full of algae and plants that some organisms can't get enough light to photosynthesise. These organisms start to die.

**1** Mineral ions (nitrates and phosphates) from fertilisers or sewage (see below) enter the water.

**4** With more food available, microorganisms that feed on these dead organisms increase in number.

**6** Aerobic organisms (ones that need oxygen to live, like fish) die because of the reduced oxygen concentration.

**5** The respiration of the microorganisms depletes (uses up) all the oxygen in the water.

## Sewage can Cause Eutrophication Too

Eutrophication can also happen because of pollution by sewage — which is anything that goes down your drains, not just stuff from the loo.

• Sewage contains lots of phosphates from detergents, e.g. washing powder.

• It also contains nitrates from urine and faeces.

These extra nutrients cause eutrophication in exactly the same way that fertilisers do.

## Eutrophication — not all big words are clever...

I bet that's properly put you off your tea. It's not a nice subject, but then it's not very nice for the ickle fishies either. Just remember — if you get asked about how humans cause pollution, you need to cover all the stuff on the last page and this one. That's a lot of stuff, so you best get learning.

# Deforestation and Destruction of Peat Bogs

Trees and peat bogs trap carbon dioxide and lock it up. The problems only start when it escapes...

## Deforestation means Chopping Down Trees

Deforestation is the cutting down of forests. This causes big problems when it's done on a large-scale, such as cutting down rainforests in tropical areas. It's done for various reasons:

1) To provide timber to use as building material.

2) To clear more land for farming, which is important to:
   • provide more food, e.g. from more rice fields or farming more cattle,
   • or, grow crops from which biofuels based on ethanol can be produced.

## Deforestation in Tropical Areas Leads to Four Main Problems

① **MORE METHANE IN THE ATMOSPHERE**

1) Rice is grown in warm, waterlogged conditions — ideal for decomposers. These organisms produce methane, so more is released into the atmosphere.

2) Cattle produce methane and rearing cattle means that more methane is released.

It's the cows' "pumping" that's the problem, believe it or not...

② **MORE CARBON DIOXIDE IN THE ATMOSPHERE**

1) Carbon dioxide is released when trees are burnt to clear land. (Carbon in wood doesn't contribute to atmospheric pollution until it's released by burning.)

2) Microorganisms feeding on bits of dead wood release carbon dioxide as a waste product of respiration.

③ **LESS CARBON DIOXIDE TAKEN IN**

Cutting down loads of trees means that the amount of carbon dioxide removed from the atmosphere during photosynthesis is reduced.

More $CO_2$ (and methane) in the atmosphere causes global warming (p. 89), which leads to climate change (p. 90).

④ **LESS BIODIVERSITY**

1) Biodiversity is the variety of different species in a habitat — more species equals greater biodiversity.

2) Habitats like tropical rainforests can contain a huge number of different species, so when they are destroyed there is a danger of many species becoming extinct — biodiversity is reduced.

3) This causes a number of lost opportunities, e.g. there are probably loads of useful products that we will never know about because the organisms that produced them have become extinct. Newly discovered plants and animals are a great source of new foods, new fibres for clothing and new medicines.

## Destroying Peat Bogs Adds More CO₂ to the Atmosphere

1) Bogs are areas of land that are acidic and waterlogged. Plants that live in bogs don't fully decay when they die, because there's not enough oxygen. The partly-rotted plants gradually build up to form peat.

2) So the carbon in the plants is stored in the peat instead of being released into the atmosphere.

3) However, peat bogs are often drained so that the area can be used as farmland, or the peat is cut up and dried to use as fuel. Peat is also sold to gardeners as compost.

4) Peat starts to decompose when the bogs are drained, so carbon dioxide is released. If we continue to destroy peat bogs, more carbon dioxide will be released, adding to the greenhouse effect (see page 89).

5) So one way people can do their bit is by buying peat free compost for their gardens (e.g. manure, leaf mould or bark chippings) to reduce the demand for peat.

## Methane is a stinky problem but an important one...

... and all that carbon dioxide is a bit of a worry too. So learn this page and make sure you know your stuff.

# Carbon Dioxide and the Greenhouse Effect

The greenhouse effect is really important. We need it, since it makes Earth a suitable temperature for living on. But unfortunately it's starting to trap more heat than is necessary. This is because there's an increasing amount of carbon dioxide and methane in the atmosphere...

## Carbon Dioxide is Removed from the Air and Stored in Various Places

1) Carbon is present in the atmosphere as carbon dioxide ($CO_2$).

2) Many processes lead to $CO_2$ being released, e.g. burning fossil fuels.

3) Too much $CO_2$ in the atmosphere causes global warming (see below).

4) Luckily, the $CO_2$ can be sequestered ('locked up') in natural stores, including:

- Oceans, lakes and ponds.
- Green plants (including trees), where it's stored as carbon compounds. Green plants remove $CO_2$ from the atmosphere during photosynthesis.
- Peat bogs (see page 88).

5) Storing $CO_2$ in these ways is really important because it means $CO_2$ is removed from the atmosphere.

## Carbon Dioxide and Methane Trap Heat from the Sun

1) The temperature of the Earth is a balance between the heat it gets from the Sun and the heat it radiates back out into space.

2) Gases in the atmosphere naturally act like an insulating layer. They absorb most of the heat that would normally be radiated out into space, and re-radiate it in all directions (including back towards the Earth).

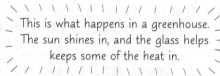
This is what happens in a greenhouse. The sun shines in, and the glass helps keeps some of the heat in.

3) If this didn't happen, then at night there'd be nothing to keep any heat in, and we'd quickly get very cold indeed. But recently we've started to worry that this effect is getting a bit out of hand...

4) There are several different gases in the atmosphere which help keep the heat in. They're called "greenhouse gases" (oddly enough) and the main ones whose levels we worry about are carbon dioxide and methane — because the levels of these two gases are rising quite sharply.

5) The Earth is gradually heating up because of the increasing levels of greenhouse gases — this is global warming. If the Earth's temperature increases by only a few °C there might be a big change in climate — there's lots more on this on the next page.

## The greenhouse effect — when you start growing into a tomato...

Global warming is rarely out of the news. Scientists accept it's happening and that human activity has caused most of the recent warming. But, they don't know exactly what the effects will be — as you'll find out next...

# Climate Change

The Earth is getting warmer. Climate scientists are now trying to work out what the effects of global warming might be — sadly, it's not as simple as everyone having nicer summers.

## The Consequences of Global Warming Could be Pretty Serious

A few measly degrees might not sound like a lot but it could have a lot of not very nice effects:

1) As the sea gets warmer, it expands, causing sea level to rise. Sea level has risen a little bit over the last 100 years. If it keeps rising it'll be bad news for people living in low-lying places like the Netherlands, East Anglia and the Maldives — they'd be flooded.

2) Higher temperatures make ice melt. Water that's currently 'trapped' on land (as ice) runs into the sea, causing sea level to rise even more.

3) Global warming also causes other changes in climate (e.g. changes to weather). It's thought that many regions will suffer more extreme weather because of this, e.g. longer, hotter droughts. Hurricanes form over water that's warmer than 27 °C — so with more warm water, you'd expect more hurricanes. However, the climate is a very complicated system. It's hard to predict exactly what will happen, but lots of people are working on it, and it's not looking too good.

4) The distribution of many wild animal and plant species may change. Some species may become more widely distributed, e.g. species that need warmer temperatures may spread further as the conditions they thrive in exist over a wider area. Other species may become less widely distributed, e.g. species that need cooler temperatures may have smaller ranges as the conditions they thrive in exist over a smaller area.

5) Biodiversity (see page 88) could be reduced if some species are unable to survive a change in the climate, so become extinct.

6) There could be changes in migration patterns too, e.g. some birds may migrate further north, as more northern areas are getting warmer.

## You Need to Weigh Up the Evidence Before Making Judgements

1) To find out how our climate is changing, scientists are busy collecting data about the environment.

2) For instance, we're using satellites to monitor snow and ice cover, and to measure the temperature of the sea surface. We're recording the temperature and speed of the ocean currents, to try and detect any changes. Automatic weather stations are constantly recording atmospheric temperatures.

3) All this data is only useful if it covers a wide enough area and a long enough time scale to make the results reliable and valid.

4) Generally, observations of a very small area aren't much use. Noticing that your local glacier seems to be melting does not mean that ice everywhere is melting, and it's certainly not a valid way to show that global temperature is changing. (That would be like going to Wales, seeing a stripy cow and concluding that all the cows in Wales are turning into zebras.) Looking at the area of ice cover over a whole continent, like Antarctica, would be better.

5) The same thing goes for time. It's no good going to the Arctic, seeing four polar bears one week but only two the next week and concluding that polar bears are dying out because the ice is disappearing. You need to do your observations again and again, year after year.

6) Scientists can make mistakes — so don't take one person's word for something, even if they've got a PhD. But if lots of scientists get the same result using different methods, it's more reliable, and so probably right. That's why most governments around the world are starting to take climate change seriously.

## Climate control — it's optional on most 4×4s...

We humans have created some big environmental problems for ourselves. Many people, and some governments, think we ought to start cleaning up the mess. Scientists can help, mainly in understanding the problems and suggesting solutions, but it's society as a whole that has to do something.

# Evolution

**THEORY OF EVOLUTION:** More than 3 billion years ago, life on Earth began as simple organisms from which all the more complex organisms evolved (rather than just popping into existence).

## All Organisms are Related... even if Only Distantly

Looking at the <u>similarities</u> and <u>differences</u> between organisms allows us to <u>classify</u> them into groups. E.g:

1) <u>Plants</u> make their <u>own food</u> (by <u>photosynthesis</u>) and are <u>fixed</u> in the ground.
2) <u>Animals</u> <u>move</u> about the place and <u>can't</u> make their own food.
3) <u>Microorganisms</u> are different to plants and animals, e.g. bacteria are <u>single-celled</u>.

Studying the similarities and differences between organisms also help us to understand how <u>all</u> living things are <u>related</u> (<u>evolutionary relationships</u>) and how they <u>interact</u> with each other (<u>ecological relationships</u>):

**EVOLUTIONARY**

1) Species with similar characteristics often have <u>similar genes</u> because they share a <u>recent common ancestor</u>, so they're <u>closely related</u>. They often look very <u>alike</u> and tend to live in similar types of <u>habitat</u>, e.g. whales and dolphins.
2) Occasionally, <u>genetically different</u> species might <u>look alike</u> too. E.g. dolphins and sharks look pretty similar because they've both <u>adapted</u> to living in the same habitat. But they're <u>not</u> <u>closely related</u> — they've evolved from <u>different ancestors</u>.
3) <u>Evolutionary trees</u> show common ancestors and relationships between organisms. The more <u>recent</u> the common ancestor, the more <u>closely related</u> the two species.

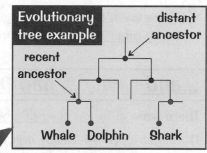

Whales and dolphins have a recent common ancestor so are closely related. They're both more distantly related to sharks.

**ECOLOGICAL**

1) If we see organisms in the same environment with <u>similar characteristics</u> (e.g. dolphins and sharks) it suggests they might be in <u>competition</u> (e.g for the same food source).
2) <u>Differences</u> between organisms in the same environment (e.g. dolphins swim in small groups, but herring swim in giant shoals) can show <u>predator-prey relationships</u> (e.g. dolphins hunt herring).

## Natural Selection Explains How Evolution Occurs

<u>Charles Darwin</u> came up with the idea of <u>evolution by natural selection</u>:

*Genetic differences are caused by sexual reproduction (see page 75) and mutations (changes to DNA).*

1) Individuals within a species show <u>variation</u> because of the <u>differences</u> in their <u>genes</u>, e.g. some rabbits have big ears and some have small ones.
2) Individuals with <u>characteristics</u> that make them <u>better adapted</u> to the environment have a <u>better chance of survival</u> and so are more likely to <u>breed</u> successfully. E.g. big-eared rabbits are more likely to hear a fox sneaking up on them, and so are more likely to live and have millions of babies. Small-eared rabbits are more likely to end up as fox food.
3) So, the <u>genes</u> that are responsible for the <u>useful characteristics</u> are more likely to be <u>passed on</u> to the <u>next generation</u>. E.g. all the baby rabbits are born with big ears.

The thing about evolution is it takes a long time. Like I mean a <u>really loooooooong time</u>. With <u>each generation</u>, <u>more individuals</u> will <u>gain</u> the <u>useful gene</u> and so the <u>characteristic</u>. But it takes <u>many, many, many generations</u> (and so a <u>very long time</u>) for the <u>gene</u> and <u>characteristic</u> to <u>accumulate</u> and <u>become normal</u> for the <u>whole population</u>. Only then will the species have <u>evolved</u> from, e.g. <u>small-eared</u> rabbits to <u>big-eared</u> rabbits.

## "Natural selection" — sounds like vegan chocolates...

Natural selection's all about the organisms with the <u>best characteristics</u> surviving to <u>pass on their genes</u> so that the whole species ends up <u>adapted</u> to its environment. It doesn't happen overnight though. It took a few million years to get from apes to us — though one or two people I know don't seem to have made it yet...

# More About Evolution

There's a lot of <u>evidence</u> for the theory of <u>evolution</u> by natural selection.
But back in the day, poor Charlie Darwin didn't have half as much evidence to convince people.

## Not Everyone Agreed with Darwin...

Darwin's idea was very <u>controversial</u> at the time — for various reasons...

① It went against common <u>religious beliefs</u> about how life on Earth developed — it was the first plausible explanation for our own existence <u>without</u> the need for a "Creator" (God).

② Darwin couldn't give a <u>good explanation</u> for why these new, useful characteristics <u>appeared</u> or exactly <u>how</u> individual organisms passed on their beneficial characteristics to their offspring. But then he didn't know anything about <u>genes</u> — they weren't discovered 'til 50 years after his theory was published.

③ There wasn't enough <u>evidence</u> to convince many <u>scientists</u>, because not many <u>other studies</u> had been done into how organisms change over time.

## ...and Lamarck had Different Ideas

There were <u>different scientific hypotheses</u> about evolution around at the same time, such as Lamarck's:

1) <u>Lamarck</u> (1744-1829) argued that if a <u>characteristic</u> was <u>used a lot</u> by an organism then it would become <u>more developed</u> during its <u>lifetime</u>. E.g. if a rabbit <u>used</u> its legs to run a lot (to escape predators), then its legs would get <u>longer</u>.

2) Lamarck believed that these <u>acquired characteristics</u> would be passed on to the <u>next generation</u>, e.g. the rabbit's offspring would have <u>longer legs</u>.

3) <u>Some evidence</u> is now coming to light that suggests a <u>tiny number</u> of characteristics might be <u>inherited a bit like this</u> — <u>changes</u> that occur to the <u>parents</u> <u>within their lifetime</u> can be inherited by <u>future generations</u>. But it's early days, and <u>we do know</u> that most of the time inheritance <u>doesn't occur like this</u>.

## Scientists can Develop Different Hypotheses from Similar Observations

1) Often scientists come up with <u>different hypotheses</u> to explain <u>similar observations</u>.
2) Scientists might develop different hypotheses because they have different <u>beliefs</u> (e.g. religious) or they have been <u>influenced</u> by different people (e.g. other scientists and their way of thinking)... or they just darn well <u>think differently</u>.

*There's more about how science works on page 1.*

3) The only way to <u>find out</u> whose hypothesis is right is to find evidence to <u>support</u> or <u>disprove</u> each one.
4) For example, Lamarck and Darwin both had different hypotheses to explain how evolution happens. In the end...

- Lamarck's hypothesis was eventually <u>rejected</u> as the <u>main way</u> evolution occurs because experiments <u>didn't support his hypothesis</u>. You can see it for yourself, e.g. if you dye a hamster's fur <u>bright pink</u> (not recommended), its offspring will still be born with the <u>normal</u> fur colour because the new characteristic <u>won't</u> have been passed on.
- The discovery of genetics <u>supported</u> Darwin's idea because it provided an <u>explanation</u> of how organisms born with beneficial characteristics can <u>pass them on</u> (i.e. via their genes).

5) There's so much evidence for Darwin's idea that it's now an <u>accepted hypothesis</u> (a <u>theory</u>).

## Did you know that exams evolved from the Spanish Inquisition...

This is a good example of how scientific hypotheses come about — someone <u>observes</u> something and then tries to <u>explain</u> it. Their hypothesis will then be <u>tested</u> by other scientists — if their evidence supports the hypothesis, it gains in credibility. If not, it's <u>rejected</u>. Darwin's theory <u>hasn't</u> been <u>rejected</u> yet.

# Fossils

Fossils are great. If they're <u>well-preserved</u>, you can see what oldy-worldy creatures <u>looked</u> like. They also show how living things have <u>evolved</u>. Although we're not sure how life started in the first place...

## Fossils are the Remains of Plants and Animals

Fossils are the <u>remains</u> of organisms from <u>many thousands of years ago</u>, which are found in <u>rocks</u>. They provide the <u>evidence</u> that organisms lived ages ago. Fossils can tell us a lot about <u>how much</u> or <u>how little organisms</u> have <u>changed</u> (<u>evolved</u>) over time. Fossils form in rocks in one of <u>three</u> ways:

### 1) FROM <u>GRADUAL REPLACEMENT</u> BY MINERALS   (Most fossils happen this way.)

1) Things like <u>teeth</u>, <u>shells</u>, <u>bones</u> etc., which <u>don't decay</u> easily, can last a long time when <u>buried</u>.

2) They're eventually <u>replaced by minerals</u> as they decay, forming a <u>rock-like substance</u> shaped like the original hard part.

3) The surrounding sediments also turn to rock, but the fossil stays <u>distinct</u> inside the rock and eventually someone <u>digs it up</u>.

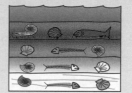

### 2) FROM <u>CASTS</u> AND <u>IMPRESSIONS</u>

1) Sometimes, fossils are formed when an organism is <u>buried</u> in a <u>soft</u> material like clay. The clay later <u>hardens</u> around it and the organism decays, leaving a <u>cast</u> of itself. An animal's <u>burrow</u> or a plant's <u>roots</u> (<u>rootlet traces</u>) can be preserved as casts.

2) Things like footprints can also be <u>pressed</u> into these materials when soft, leaving an <u>impression</u> when it hardens.

### 3) FROM <u>PRESERVATION</u> IN PLACES WHERE NO DECAY HAPPENS

1) In <u>amber</u> (a clear yellow 'stone' made from fossilised resin) and <u>tar pits</u> there's no <u>oxygen</u> or <u>moisture</u> so <u>decay microbes</u> can't survive.

2) In <u>glaciers</u> it's too <u>cold</u> for the <u>decay microbes</u> to work.

3) <u>Peat bogs</u> are too <u>acidic</u> for <u>decay microbes</u>.
(A fully preserved man they named 'Pete Marsh' was found in a bog.)

## But No One Knows How Life Began

Fossils show how much or how little different organisms have changed (<u>evolved</u>) as life has developed on Earth over millions of years. But where did the <u>first</u> living thing come from...

1) There are various <u>hypotheses</u> suggesting how life first came into being, but no one really <u>knows</u>.

2) Maybe the first life forms came into existence in a primordial <u>swamp</u> (or under the <u>sea</u>) here on <u>Earth</u>. Maybe simple organic molecules were brought to Earth on <u>comets</u> — these could have then become more <u>complex</u> organic molecules, and eventually very simple <u>life forms</u>.

3) These hypotheses can't be supported or disproved because there's a <u>lack</u> of good, <u>valid</u> evidence:

- Many early forms of life were <u>soft-bodied</u>, and soft tissue tends to decay away <u>completely</u> — so the fossil record is <u>incomplete</u>.

- Fossils that did form millions of years ago may have been <u>destroyed</u> by <u>geological activity</u>, e.g. the movement of tectonic plates may have crushed fossils already formed in the rock.

Validity is explained on page 2.

## Don't get bogged down by all this information...

It's a bit mind-boggling really, how <u>fossils</u> of organisms can still exist even millions of years after they died. Right, testing time... scribble down the <u>three ways</u> that fossils form and why we can't be sure <u>how life began</u>.

# Extinction and Speciation

Evolution leads to the development of lots of <u>different species</u>.  But not every species is still around today... :(

## Extinction Happens if You Can't Evolve Quickly Enough

The fossil record contains many species that <u>don't exist any more</u> — these species are said to be <u>extinct</u>.
<u>Dinosaurs</u> and <u>mammoths</u> are extinct animals, with only <u>fossils</u> to tell us they existed at all.

Species become extinct for these reasons:
1) The <u>environment changes</u> too quickly (e.g. destruction of habitat).
2) A <u>new predator</u> kills them all (e.g. humans hunting them).
3) A <u>new disease</u> kills them all.
4) They can't <u>compete</u> with another (new) species for <u>food</u>.
5) A <u>catastrophic event</u> happens that kills them all
   (e.g. a volcanic eruption or a collision with an asteroid).
6) A <u>new species</u> develops (this is called speciation — see below).

Dodos are now extinct.  Humans not only hunted them, but introduced other animals which ate all their eggs, and we destroyed the forest where they lived — they really didn't stand a chance...

## Speciation is the Development of a New Species

1) A species is a group of <u>similar organisms</u> that can <u>reproduce</u> to give <u>fertile offspring</u>.
2) <u>Speciation</u> is the development of a <u>new species</u>.
3) Speciation occurs when <u>populations</u> of the <u>same species</u> become so <u>different</u> that they can <u>no longer breed</u> together to produce <u>fertile offspring</u>.

## Isolation and Natural Selection Lead to Speciation

<u>Isolation</u> is where <u>populations</u> of a species are <u>separated</u>.  This can happen due to a <u>physical barrier</u>.
E.g. floods and earthquakes can cause barriers that <u>geographically isolate</u> some individuals from the main population.  <u>Conditions</u> on either side of the barrier will be <u>slightly different</u>, e.g. they may have <u>different climates</u>.  Because the environment is <u>different</u> on each side, <u>different characteristics</u> will become more common in each population due to <u>natural selection</u>:

1) Each population shows <u>genetic variation</u> because they have a wide range of <u>alleles</u>.
2) In each population, individuals with characteristics that make them better adapted to their environment have a <u>better chance of survival</u> and so are more likely to <u>breed</u> successfully.
3) So the <u>alleles</u> that control the <u>beneficial characteristics</u> are more likely to be <u>passed on</u> to the <u>next generation</u>.

Eventually, individuals from the different populations will have <u>changed</u> so much that they <u>won't</u> be able to <u>breed</u> with one another to produce fertile offspring.  The two groups will have become <u>separate species</u>.

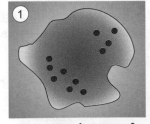 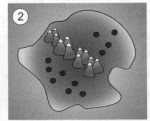 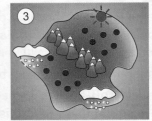 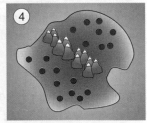

Two populations of the same species
● = individual organism
⟹ Physical barriers separate populations.
⟹ Populations adapt to new environments.
⟹ Development of a new species.

## Up for grabs — a top quality gag about speciation...going once...going twice...

So <u>speciation</u> happens if two or more populations of the same species change so much that they can <u>no longer breed together</u> to produce <u>fertile offspring</u>.  It's caused by the populations becoming <u>separated</u> from each other.  Right, I think it must be nearly time for a tea break before our brain cells become extinct...

# Pyramids of Biomass

And now for something slightly different... A <u>trophic level</u> is a <u>feeding</u> level. It comes from the Greek word <u>trophe</u> meaning 'nourishment'. So there.

## You Need to Be Able to Construct Pyramids of Biomass

There's <u>less energy</u> and <u>less biomass</u> every time you move <u>up</u> a stage (<u>trophic level</u>) in a food chain. There are usually <u>fewer organisms</u> every time you move up a level too:

*Biomass just means the mass of living material.*

100 dandelions... feed... 10 rabbits... which feed... one fox.

This <u>isn't</u> always true though — for example, if <u>500 fleas</u> are feeding on the fox, the number of organisms has <u>increased</u> as you move up that stage in the food chain. So a better way to look at the food chain is often to think about <u>biomass</u> instead of number of organisms. You can use information about biomass to construct a <u>pyramid of biomass</u> to represent the food chain:

1) Each bar on a <u>pyramid of biomass</u> shows the <u>mass of living material</u> at that stage of the food chain — basically how much all the organisms at each level would "<u>weigh</u>" if you put them <u>all together</u>.

2) So the one fox above would have a <u>big biomass</u> and the <u>hundreds of fleas</u> would have a <u>very small biomass</u>. Biomass pyramids are practically <u>always pyramid-shaped</u>:

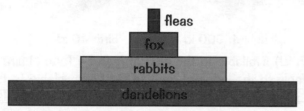

You need to be able to <u>construct</u> pyramids of biomass. Luckily it's pretty simple — they'll give you <u>all</u> the <u>information</u> you need to do it in the exam.

The big bar along the bottom of the pyramid always represents the <u>producer</u> (i.e. a plant).
The next bar will be the <u>primary consumer</u> (the animal that eats the plant), then the <u>secondary consumer</u> (the animal that eats the primary consumer) and so on up the food chain. Easy.

## You Need to be Able to Interpret Pyramids of Biomass

You also need to be able to look at pyramids of biomass and <u>explain</u> what they show about the <u>food chain</u>. Also very easy — just remember, the <u>biomass</u> at <u>each stage</u> should be <u>drawn to scale</u>. For example:

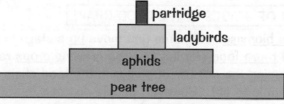

Even if you know nothing about the natural world, you're probably aware that a <u>tree</u> is quite a bit <u>bigger</u> than an <u>aphid</u>. So what's going on here is that <u>lots</u> (probably thousands) of aphids are feeding on a <u>few</u> great big trees. Quite a lot of <u>ladybirds</u> are then eating the aphids, and a few <u>partridges</u> are eating the ladybirds. <u>Biomass</u> and <u>energy</u> are still <u>decreasing</u> as you go up the levels — it's just that <u>one tree</u> can have a very <u>big biomass</u>, and can fix a lot of the <u>Sun's energy</u> using all those leaves.
If you're given <u>actual numbers</u>, <u>use them</u> to <u>draw bars</u> of the <u>correct scale</u>.

## Constructing pyramids is a breeze — just ask the Egyptians...

There are actually a couple of exceptions where pyramids of <u>biomass</u> aren't quite pyramid-shaped. It happens when the <u>producer</u> has a <u>very short life</u> but <u>reproduces loads</u>, like with <u>plankton</u> at certain times of year. But it's very <u>rare</u>, so forget I ever mentioned it. Sorry.

# Energy Transfer

So now you need to learn **why** there's **less biomass** and **energy** each time you move up a trophic level.

## All That Energy Just Disappears Somehow...

1) Energy from the **Sun** is the source of energy for **nearly all** life on Earth.

2) **Green plants** and **algae** use **light energy** from the Sun to make **food** (glucose) during **photosynthesis**. The **amount** of energy **absorbed** that is **actually used** to **make glucose** is **very small** because some energy is **transmitted through the leaves**, some energy is lost **heating up the leaves** and some is **absorbed by non-photosynthetic parts of the leaves**. The **glucose** (chemical energy) that's made is **stored** in the substances which make up the **cells** of plants and algae, and then works its way **through the food chain** as animals **eat** them and each other.

3) **Respiration** supplies the energy for all life processes, including **movement**. Most of the energy is eventually **lost** to the surroundings as **heat**. This is especially true for **mammals** and **birds**, whose bodies must be kept at a **constant temperature** which is normally higher than their surroundings.

4) Some material that makes up plants and animals is **inedible** (e.g. bone), so it **isn't passed** to the next stage of the food chain. **Material** and **energy** are also lost from the food chain in the organisms' **waste materials**.

5) This explains why you get **biomass pyramids** — most biomass is lost, so **doesn't** get to the **next level up**.

6) It also explains why you hardly ever get **food chains** with more than about **five trophic levels**. So much **energy** is **lost** at each stage that there's not enough left to support organisms after that many stages.

7) You might have to **interpret data** on **energy flow**:

Material (biomass) and energy are both lost at each stage of the food chain.

rosebush: 80 000 kJ  greenfly: 10 000 kJ  ladybird: 900 kJ  bird: 40 kJ

The numbers show the **amount of energy** (in kJ) available to the **next stage** of a food chain. So **10 000 kJ** is the amount of energy available to the **ladybird**, and **900 kJ** is available to the **bird**. You can work out the **proportion** of energy **transferred** from **one stage** to the **next** using this **equation**:

$$\text{proportion of energy transferred} = \frac{\text{energy available to the next stage}}{\text{energy that was available to the previous stage}}$$

So the **proportion** of energy transferred from the **greenfly** to the **ladybird** = 900 kJ ÷ 10 000 kJ
= **0.09**

## The "Efficiency" of Food Production Can Be Improved by...

### 1) REDUCING THE NUMBER OF STAGES IN THE FOOD CHAIN

There's **less energy** and **less biomass** every time you move **up** a stage in a **food chain**. So for a **given area of land**, you can produce a lot **more food** (for humans) by growing **crops** rather than by having **grazing animals**. This is because you are **reducing** the number of **stages** in the food chain — only **10%** of what beef cattle eat becomes **useful meat** for people to eat. However, people do need to eat a **varied diet** to stay healthy, and there's still a lot of **demand** for meat products. Also, some land is **unsuitable** for growing crops, e.g. **moorland** or **hillsides**. In these places, animals like **sheep** and **deer** might be the **best** way to get food from the land.

### 2) RESTRICTING THE ENERGY LOST BY FARM ANIMALS

In countries like the UK, animals such as **pigs** and **chickens** are often **intensively farmed**. They're kept **close together indoors** in small pens, so that they're **warm** and **can't move about**. Restricting **movement** and **heat loss** saves **energy**. It makes the **transfer of energy** from the animal feed to the animal more **efficient** — so basically, the animals will **grow faster** on **less food**. This makes things **cheaper** for the **farmer**, and for **us**.

## Locked in a little cage with no sunlight — who'd work in a bank...

You may well have a **strong opinion** on the intensive farming of animals — whether it's 'tree-hugging hippies, just give me a bit of cheap pork,' or 'poor creatures, they should be free!' Either way, you still need to **learn this**.

# Problems with Food Production and Distribution

Modern ways of producing and distributing food have advantages but also disadvantages.

## Efficient Food Production Involves Compromises and Conflict

Improving the efficiency of food production is useful — it means cheaper food for us, and better standards of living for farmers. It also helps to feed an increasing human population. But it all comes at a cost.

There are a lot of arguments against factory farming:

1) Some people think that forcing animals to live in unnatural and uncomfortable conditions is cruel. There's a growing demand for organic meat, which means the animals will not have been intensively farmed.

2) The crowded conditions on factory farms create a favourable environment for the spread of diseases, like avian flu and foot-and-mouth disease.

3) To try to prevent disease, animals are given antibiotics. When the animals are eaten these can enter humans. This allows microbes that infect humans to develop immunity to those antibiotics — so the antibiotics become less effective as human medicines.

4) The animals need to be kept warm to reduce the energy they lose as heat. This often means using power from fossil fuels — which we wouldn't be using if the animals were grazing in their natural environment.

5) Our fish stocks are getting low (see below). Yet a lot of fish goes on feeding animals that are intensively farmed — these animals wouldn't usually eat this source of food.

## Food Distribution Also Causes Problems

Some food products have lots of 'food miles' — they're transported a long way from where they're produced to where they're sold, e.g. some green beans you buy in the UK have come from Kenya.

This can be expensive and it's also bad for the environment. Planes, ships and trucks all burn scarce fossil fuels and release carbon dioxide into the atmosphere, contributing to global warming.

## Overfishing is Decreasing Fish Stocks

1) Fish stocks are declining because we're fishing so much.

2) This means there's less fish for us to eat, the ocean's food chains are affected and some species of fish may disappear altogether in some areas.

3) To tackle this problem, we need to maintain fish stocks at a level where the fish continue to breed. This is sustainable food production — having enough food without using resources faster than they renew.

4) Fish stocks can be maintained (conserved) in these ways:

**FISHING QUOTAS** — there are limits on the number and size of fish that can be caught in certain areas. This prevents certain species from being overfished.

**NET SIZE** — there are different limits of the mesh size of the fish net, depending on what's being fished. This is to reduce the number of 'unwanted' and discarded fish — the ones that are accidently caught, e.g. shrimp caught along with cod. Using a bigger mesh size will let the 'unwanted' species escape. It also means that younger fish will slip through the net, allowing them to reach breeding age.

## Fishermen are just too effishent... (groan...)

In an exam, you may be asked to give an account of the positive and negative aspects of efficient food production. You'll need to put both sides, whatever your personal opinion is. If you get given some information on a particular case, make sure you use it — they want to see that you've read it carefully.

# Decay and the Carbon Cycle

Recycling may be a buzz word for us but it's old school for nature. All the <u>nutrients</u> in our environment are constantly being <u>recycled</u> — there's a nice balance between what <u>goes in</u> and what <u>goes out</u> again.

## Elements are Cycled Back to the Start of the Food Chain by Decay

1) <u>Living things</u> are made of materials they take from the world around them. E.g. <u>plants</u> turn elements like <u>carbon</u>, <u>oxygen</u>, <u>hydrogen</u> and <u>nitrogen</u> from the <u>soil</u> and the <u>air</u> into the <u>complex compounds</u> (carbohydrates, proteins and fats) that make up living organisms. These get passed up the <u>food chain</u>.

2) These materials are <u>returned</u> to the environment in <u>waste products</u>, or when the organisms <u>die</u> and <u>decay</u>.

3) Materials decay because they're <u>broken down</u> (digested) by <u>microorganisms</u>. This happens faster in <u>warm</u>, <u>moist</u>, <u>aerobic</u> (oxygen rich) conditions because microorganisms are more active in these conditions.

4) <u>Decay</u> puts the stuff that plants need to grow (see point 1) <u>back</u> into the <u>soil</u>.

5) In a <u>stable community</u>, the materials that are <u>taken out</u> of the soil and <u>used</u> by plants etc. are <u>balanced</u> by those that are put <u>back in</u>. There's a constant <u>cycle</u> happening.

## The Constant Cycling of Carbon is called the Carbon Cycle

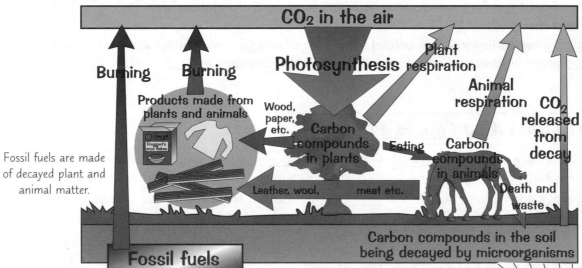

That can look a bit complicated at first, but it's actually pretty simple.
<u>Learn</u> these important points:

The <u>energy</u> that green plants and algae get from photosynthesis is <u>transferred up</u> the food chain.

1) <u>CO$_2$</u> is removed from the <u>atmosphere</u> by green plants and algae during <u>photosynthesis</u>. The carbon is used to make the <u>carbohydrates</u>, <u>fats</u> and <u>proteins</u> that make up the <u>bodies</u> of the plants and algae.

2) When the <u>plants and algae respire</u>, some carbon is <u>returned</u> to the atmosphere as CO$_2$.

3) When the plants and algae are <u>eaten</u> by <u>animals</u>, some carbon becomes part of the <u>fats</u> and <u>proteins</u> in their bodies. The carbon then moves through the <u>food chain</u>.

4) When the <u>animals respire</u>, some carbon is <u>returned</u> to the atmosphere as CO$_2$.

5) When plants, algae and animals <u>die</u>, other animals (called <u>detritus feeders</u>) and <u>microorganisms</u> feed on their remains. When these organisms <u>respire</u>, CO$_2$ is <u>returned</u> to the atmosphere.

6) <u>Animals</u> also produce <u>waste</u> that is <u>broken down</u> by <u>detritus feeders</u> and <u>microorganisms</u>.

7) The <u>combustion</u> (burning) of wood and fossil fuels, also <u>releases CO$_2$</u> back into the air.

8) So the <u>carbon</u> (and <u>energy</u>) is constantly being <u>cycled</u> — from the <u>air</u>, through <u>food chains</u> (via <u>plants</u>, <u>algae</u> and <u>animals</u>, and <u>detritus feeders</u> and <u>microorganisms</u>) and eventually back out into the <u>air</u> again.

## What goes around comes around...

Carbon is very <u>important</u> for living things — it's the basis for all the <u>organic molecules</u> (fats, proteins, carbohydrates, etc.) in our bodies. In sci-fi films the aliens are sometimes <u>silicon-based</u>... but then by the end they've usually been defeated by some Bruce Willis type, so I don't really think they're onto a winner.

# Revision Summary for Section Nine

That was a fairly big section, so well done. It was also the last section — huzzah! But don't get too excited cos we ain't done with it just yet. These questions are designed to really test whether you know all your stuff — ignore them at your peril. OK, rant over — I'll leave it to you...

1)   What is happening to the world's population?  What is largely responsible for this trend?

2)   Suggest three ways in which a rising population is affecting the environment.

3)   What are the four main activities that use up land?

4)   What is eutrophication?  How does it kill fish?

5)   Give two reasons why people chop down large areas of forest.

6)   What is biodiversity?  Describe how deforestation can lead to a reduction in biodiversity.

7)   Apart from a reduction in biodiversity, what three other problems can deforestation lead to?

8)   Explain why using peat-free compost is better for the environment than using peat.

9)   Name five important stores of carbon.

10)  Why is it so important to have stores of carbon?

11)  Name two important greenhouse gases.  Why are they called 'greenhouse' gases?

12)  Draw and label a diagram to explain the greenhouse effect.

13)  Describe three possible consequences of global warming.

14)* Read the statement below and consider how valid it is.

> The Malaspina Glacier in Alaska is losing over 2.7 km³ of water each year.
> This proves that global warming is happening.

15)  What do evolutionary trees show?

16)  Explain Darwin's theory of evolution by natural selection.

17)  Why was Darwin's idea very controversial at the time?

18)  Explain how Lamarck's hypothesis was different from Darwin's.

19)  Describe the three ways that fossils can form.  Give an example of each type.

20)  Give three reasons why some species become extinct.

21)  What is speciation?  Explain how geographical isolation can lead to speciation.

22)  What does each bar on a pyramid of biomass represent?

23)  Give two ways that energy is lost from a food chain.

24)  A farmer has a field.  He plans to grow corn in it and then feed the corn to his cows, which he raises for meat.  How could the farmer use the field more efficiently to produce food for humans?

25)  Why do chickens kept in tiny cages in heated sheds need less food?

26)  Summarise the main arguments against efficient food production.

27)  Give two ways that fish stocks can be conserved.

28)  Give one way that carbon dioxide from the air enters a food chain.

29)  Give three ways that carbon compounds in a food chain become carbon dioxide in the air again.

* Answer on page 100.

# Index and Answers

## Answers